FOREWORD

The outdoor world, as most of you know, is an unusual place filled with fascinating events. A special sunrise. A flushing grouse. A noble buck. Well, you get the idea.

Fate also seems to roam the fields and forests.

Although I first met Chef John Schumacher on a fishing trip, my fondest memories of our friendship occurred on a sun-stroked mountainside amid the ponderosa pines of the Black Hills. It was just a few minutes past sunrise when Chef John and I shared a special moment with one of the grandest gamebirds in the world, the wild turkey.

Yes, Chef John "cooled" that bird for a turkey dinner, but not before we witnessed one of nature's finest spring moments, the gobble and courtship of a wild tom turkey.

On that special morning, that ol' gobbler cemented Chef John's admiration for wild turkey hunting, and it launched a long friendship between Chef John and me.

We didn't understand at the time, but we had shared a moment in the woods that would bond us as friends for the rest of our lives. Today, Chef John is the real "game gourmet." He's walked the game trails, he's heard the elk bugle at dusk, and I know he's heard the music of wild turkeys at the crack of dawn.
Plus, he can cook.

He's no greenhorn. Chef John is a hunter who understands the responsibilities of gathering game and maintaining wild places for wild game to prosper.

When my television show, Minnesota Bound, was young, we wanted to show our audience that we are all hunters in one way or another. Some of us hunt in the supermarket. Some of us hunt in nature's market. We wanted to show that hunting was not killing, but a continuation of the cycle of life. If we hunted a deer, we wanted viewers to know it was game that could sustain our bodies as it has for centuries.

Chef John knows how to bring out the best in nature's finest and most natural of all food, wild game. And he knows how to teach the rest of us to head for the woods for "good eatin."

Best regards,
Ron Schara, host
Minnesota Bound television show

Dear Readers,

The recipes in this book have all been presented on the ***Minnesota Bound & Backroads with Ron and Raven*** *television shows and in some of my other cookbooks and cooking videos.*

They are the personal favorites that I take on camping, hunting and fishing trips.

These recipes were chosen because they are easy to prepare and the ingredients are basic and readily available.

Good Eatin'
Chef John Schumacher

FOOD HANDLING AND SAFETY TIPS FOR THE TRIP

1. Safe drinking water has over the years become more and more important. Never trust your taste, smell or sight or how far you are from civilization for safe drinking water. Water contamination comes from all sources: chemical, mineral, animal and human wastes.
2. Drink bottled water if possible. To be extra safe, drink carbonated water (especially in North America). Carbon dioxide brings the water acid to 4.2 which kills bacteria.
3. Bring water to a boil for longer than 5 minutes. To be extra safe, boil water 25 minutes at a slow rolling boil.
4. When using bleach to purify water, add 1 teaspoon per gallon and let set for at least 1 hour.
5. Make sure to use a name brand water purification kit.
6. To purify water using pure lemon juice or vinegar, use 1 cup per gallon. Let sit 1 hour.
7. If camping, make sure the outhouse is as far from camp as possible.
8. Wash your hands thoroughly with a brush.
9. Hold all cooked foods above 150° or keep them below 40°.
10. Do not poke potatoes or vegetables with a fork. This will contaminate the inside of the vegetable.
11. Never roast potatoes in foil. Potatoes are grown in dirt. That is a source of botulism.
12. When camping, use herbed salad dressing as a marinade to fuse flavors. It has vinegar in it which will bring the pH to 4.1.
13. There are 16 kinds of E Coli. You must cook all ground meat to at least 155° or higher which is medium well to well done.
14. Be careful of bird droppings. They are just as dangerous as rodent droppings.
15. Make sure all boxes, coolers and pails are clean on the bottom.
16. 1 out of every 20,000 egg yolks has salmonella. Make scrambled eggs well cooked.
17. Wash all fruits with stems with warm water not cold because cold water will cause vegetables to absorb bacteria into the stem end.
18. Be very careful of salad greens. Wash them well.
19. Quinine or tonic water is very safe to drink. That is why the English started drinking gin and tonics in Africa.

20. Never use sponges. They are a place for germs to grow.

21. When packing for camp, keep meats, dairy and vegetables in separate bags as they may contaminate each other.

22. Do not take doggy bags from restaurants.

23. Always clean all equipment and knives after cutting especially after cutting fowl or poultry. Wash with a vinegar or bleach solution. Soap only cuts grease. It does not kill germs unless it states on the label that it is anti-bacteria soap.

24. I suggest washing everything as close to cooking as possible. Cook as close to eating as possible. When camping, try not to have leftovers as refrigeration is limited.

25. For coolers, use sealed freezer packs or sealed containers of frozen ice as melted ice spreads germs.

26. Never eat yellow snow.

GAME RECIPES

1. Game Medallions in Bacon Crust on Barbecue Caramelized Onions
2. Game Stroganoff
3. Wild Game Pizza
4. Game Breakfast Sausages
5. Kabobs That Work
6. Braised Rabbit or Squirrel
7. Game Cheeseburger Soup
8. Spicy Game Soup
9. Game Pilaf
10. Old-Fashioned Game Pot Roast
11. Grilled Game Burgers
12. Game BLT Sandwich
13. Game Hash
14. Game Porcupine Meatballs
15. Game Goulash
16. Brown Beer Crumbled Burgers
17. Game Scalloppine
18. Game Cutlets

UPLAND GAME RECIPES

WATERFOWL RECIPES

SIDE DISH RECIPES

Game Recipes

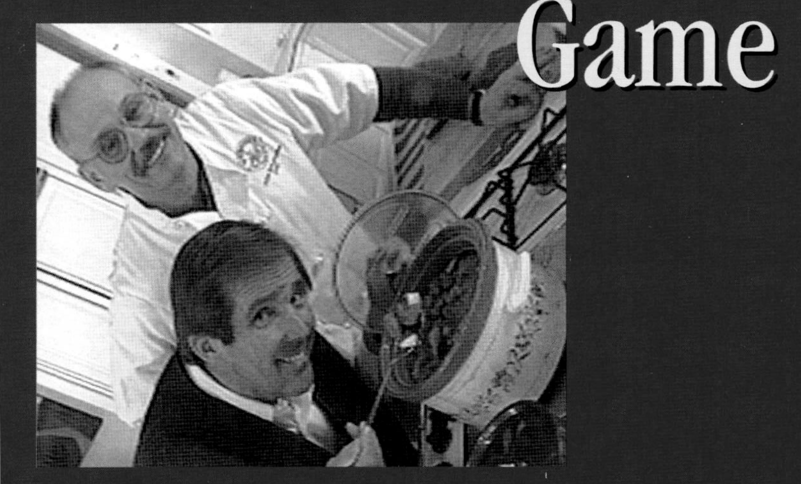

GAME MEDALLIONS in BACON CRUST on BBQ CARAMELIZED ONIONS

Trim fat and silver skin off venison roast. Place in a glass bowl. Cover with herb dressing. Cover bowl and let set for 72 hours in refrigerator. Remove and cut into 2" thick steaks. Wrap in bacon. Fasten bacon with a toothpick.

Peel and slice onions in thin slices. Place butter and onions in a heavy sauce pot on medium heat and simmer for 30 minutes. Add barbecue sauce, beer, brown sugar and paprika. Reduce heat. Simmer for 10 more minutes. Stir with a wooden spoon to keep from sticking.

Heat a heavy fry pan until hot. Add vegetable oil. Add steaks and brown well. Turn and brown other side. Cook to desired doneness. Splash with Worcestershire sauce. On a hot serving plate place caramelized onions. Top with steaks and serve.

Chef John's Tips

- For grilling steaks, make sure to use medium heat. If fire or coals are too hot, bacon will burn. Do not put barbecue sauce on tenderloin until cooked to desired doneness. The sugar in the barbecue sauce will burn before the steaks are cooked.
- If you are not a fan of beer, use water.
- This works equally well on all red game meat as well as domestic meats.
- Do not put salt on tenderloin as it draws out the juices.
- The reason for wrapping the tenderloins in bacon is to add flavor as well as keeping the steak's juices.

Game Medallions in Bacon Crust on BBQ Caramelized Onions Ingredients

- 2 lbs. boneless venison roast, cut into steaks
- 1 pint herb dressing
- 8 strips bacon
- 1/4 cup butter
- 4 cups onion, sliced thin
- 1/3 cup barbecue sauce
- 1/2 cup beer
- 2 tsp. brown sugar
- 1/4 tsp. paprika
- 1/4 cup vegetable oil
- 1 tsp. Worcestershire sauce

SERVES: 4 to 6

GAME STROGANOFF

Remove all fat and silver skin from game. Slice into 2 oz. slices. Flatten with a meat mallet. Place flour, salt, and white pepper in a pie plate and mix to combine. Place game slices into flour and coat. Shake off excess flour. Set aside.

Place butter in a large frying pan and bring to a fast bubble. Add game slices and cook for 1 minute. Turn and cook other side for 1 minute. Add shallots and mushrooms and cook for 1 minute. Add sherry wine, brown sauce and sour cream. Simmer on low heat for 10 minutes. Serve with rice, wild rice or egg noodles.

Chef John's Tips

- It's not my first choice but it is alright to use canned brown sauce or gravy.
- This recipe also works well with duck or goose breasts.
- If you are preparing for a camping trip, place in a resealable plastic bag. Mix 1/2 cup non-dairy powder and 1/4 cup non-fat dry milk powder. Add 1 cup cold water to make cream for stroganoff.

Game Stroganoff Ingredients

- 12 pieces sliced game (1-2 oz. each)
- 1 cup seasoned flour (see recipe)
- 1/2 tsp. salt
- 1/4 tsp. white pepper
- 1/4 cup clarified butter (see recipe)
- 1/2 cup shallots or red onions, diced 1/4" cubes
- 8 fresh mushrooms, cut in quarters
- 2/3 cup sherry wine
- 2 cups brown sauce (see recipe)
- 1 cup sour cream

WILD GAME PIZZA

Cut red and green peppers into 1/3" rings or slices. Cut mushrooms into fourths. Cut zucchini into 1/3" rounds. In a larger frying pan heat 1 ounce olive oil or vegetable oil. Add vegetables and sauté until almost tender. Remove from heat to a large bowl to keep. Add ground wild game meat to the hot pan and cook until done. Drain off excess fat.

Lightly grease one sheet pan or cookie sheet. Spread out the pizza dough crust into a rectangle. Spread 1 cup pizza sauce on top. Top sauce with vegetables. Spread out evenly. Remove stem ends of tomatoes and slice tomatoes into 6 slices. Top vegetables with sliced tomatoes. Place cooked wild game meat on top of this. Pour 2 cups pizza sauce over the top. Top this with venison sausage and olives. Spread toppings out evenly. Top with Mozzarella cheese. Place roasted garlic bulb in center.

Place pizza in a 375° oven for 30 minutes. Cut into six pieces and serve.

Chef John's Tips

- If you wish, you can place crust on a broiler or grill and brown it on both sides before adding the pizza ingredients. Make sure you spray the rack with a non-stick vegetable spray before browning crust.
- Ground pheasant works well in this recipe also.
- If you don't have a pizza crust mix, use potatoes. Slice potatoes thin with a potato peeler as if you were peeling the skin off. Place slices in cold salted water with 1 teaspoon lemon juice or vinegar. To prepare using potatoes, line a sheet pan, pizza pan or large shallow fry pan with foil. Brush olive oil or soft butter over foil. Lift potatoes from water. Let drain for 1 to 2 minutes. Place potato slices evenly to form a crust. Press with the back of your hand to make a tight crust.

Ingredients

- *1 cup red pepper*
- *1 cup green pepper*
- *2 cups fresh mushrooms*
- *1 1/2 cups zucchini*
- *1 oz. olive or vegetable oil*
- *2 cups ground venison, elk, caribou (red game meat)*
- *1 rollout pizza dough crust*
- *3 cups pizza sauce*
- *2 tomatoes, sliced 1/2" thick*
- *2 cups venison sausage links, 1/4" thick*
- *1 cup olives (black or green), sliced 1/4" thick*
- *2 cups Mozzarella Cheese*
- *1 bulb roasted garlic (see recipe)*

SERVES: 4 to 6

GAME BREAKFAST SAUSAGES

If you are grinding your own venison, remove fat, excessive silver skin and sinews. Chill venison to almost frozen. This makes the soft venison grind better.

In a large bowl, combine bread crumbs, thyme, salt and pepper. Add ground venison, pork sausage and egg. Mix well to combine, making sure there are no dry bread crumb spots. Rub a little oil on your hands to make patties. Make patties about 4 - 6 ounces. Press patty to 1/3" thick. Pan fry slowly until patties are cooked thoroughly. Drain off fat as patties cook.

Chef John's Tips

- Applesauce serves as a nice accompaniment.
- For sandwiches: I top these on the grill with Swiss cheese or pineapple rings and serve with bacon, lettuce and tomato on a hard roll.
- This is the best way to use ground game.
- You can freeze patties after making by placing on wax paper or plastic wrap.
- Use any flavor pork sausage you wish to change the flavor. Add your favorite spices or peppers.

Game Breakfast Sausages
Ingredients

- 1 lb. ground venison
- 1 lb. bulk pork sausage
- 1/4 cup fresh bread crumbs (see recipe)
- 1 tsp. thyme leaves
- 1 tsp. onion salt
- 1 tsp. black pepper, freshly ground
- 1 beaten egg
- oil

SERVES: 4 to 6

KABOBS that WORK

Cube meat. Place in a glass or stainless steel bowl. Cover with herb dressing and refrigerate for approximately 72 hours. Cut stems from mushrooms and simmer in sherry wine until tender. Remove liquid and keep. Set mushrooms aside. Peel and blanch onions in 1 quart salted water until tender. Drain off the liquid and set onions aside. Bring 1 quart salted water to boil. Add peppers. When water returns to a boil, remove the peppers and set aside. Remove skin from pineapple and cut into large cubes making sure not to use the core. Slice zucchini. Place items on skewers as listed below:

mushroom • onion • meat • red/green pepper • zucchini • meat •pineapple • meat • zucchini • red/green pepper • meat • onion • mushroom

Place on a medium grill (not too hot). Grill until meat and vegetables are done to your liking. While grilling, combine 1 cup meat marinade and liquid from the mushrooms and baste over the skewers.

Chef John's Tips

- Use any game or red meat.
- For fresh pineapple, split pineapple in half and cut the pineapple chunks from the skin with a grapefruit knife.
- Use any vegetables you like. Remember to precook them first.

Ingredients

- *16 - 2" cubes of game meat*
- *1 pint bottled herb dressing*
- *8 jumbo fresh mushrooms*
- *1 cup sherry wine*
- *8 pearl onions or shallots, peeled*
- *8 - 2" cubes of red/green peppers*
- *8 cubes of fresh pineapple*
- *8 slices zucchini (1/2" thick)*
- *4 - 12" bamboo or metal skewers*

SERVES: 4

BRAISED RABBIT or SQUIRREL

Clean, skin and cut each rabbit or squirrel into 6 pieces. Remove all fat and sinews.

Place flour, salt and pepper in pie plate and toss to combine. Heat oil to about 375° in an electric fry pan. Dredge pieces in flour. Place in oil and brown. Remove to Dutch oven. Place game, onions, chicken stock, wine, tomato purée, chocolate and sachet bag in pan and bake at 375° for 2 1/2 to 3 hours checking for doneness after 2 hours. Meat is tender when pressed with a fork and it separates from the bone.

To thicken sauce, remove meat to a covered dish. Strain liquid and return to pan. Add roux. Heat to a slow bubble and simmer for 15 minutes. Return meat to pan and cook until meat is hot.

Chef John's Tips

- To make mushroom sauce, add 2 cups sliced fresh mushrooms.
- I sometimes add 2/3 cup sliced green olives.

Braised Rabbit or Squirrel Ingredients

- 2 rabbits or squirrels, each cut into 6 pieces
- 1 cup seasoned flour (see recipe)
- 1 Tbsp. salt
- 1 tsp. black pepper
- 1 cup vegetable oil
- 1 1/2 cups onions, cut in 1/2" cubes
- 1 quart chicken stock (see recipe)
- 2 cups red wine
- 1/4 cup tomato purée
- 1 tsp. bittersweet chocolate
- 1 sachet bag (see recipe)
- 1/4 cup roux (see recipe)

SERVES: 4

GAME CHEESEBURGER SOUP

In a large soup pot, heat oil very hot. Cook ground game meat, garlic, onions, celery and cook until vegetables are tender and meat is brown. Stir in flour. Continue to cook on low heat for two minutes stirring occasionally.

Add beef stock, Worcestershire sauce, Tabasco sauce, ketchup, salt and pepper. Simmer for 30 minutes on low heat. Serve in bowls topped with cheese, green onions and pickles.

Chef John's Tips

- You can add diced tomatoes and sour cream.
- Instead of olive oil, use 1/2 pound of diced bacon browned

Game Cheeseburger Soup Ingredients

- *1/4 cup olive oil*
- *1 1/2 lbs. ground red game meat*
- *3 cloves minced garlic*
- *2 cups onions, diced 1/4"*
- *1 cup celery, sliced 1/4"*
- *2 Tbsp. all-purpose flour*
- *4 cups beef stock (see recipe)*
- *1 tsp. Worcestershire sauce*
- *1/4 tsp. Tabasco sauce*
- *1 cup ketchup*
- *2 tsp. salt*
- *1 1/2 tsp. freshly ground black pepper*
- *2 cups shredded cheddar cheese*
- *1 cup chopped green onions*
- *1 cup chopped dill pickles*

SERVES: 4 to 6

SPICY GAME SOUP

In a sauce pan, brown pork and antelope. Add onions and garlic and cook 5 minutes stirring occasionally to keep from sticking. Add beef stock. Simmer for 10 minutes. Skim all fat from the top. Add remaining ingredients and simmer for 30 minutes on low. Add seasoning to desired taste and serve with tortilla.

Chef John's Tips

- This goes with all red game meat.
- If you like red hot food, add extra peppers or pepper sauce

Spicy Game Soup Ingredients

- 1 cup ground pork
- 2 cups ground antelope
- 2 cups onions, cut in 1/2" cubes
- 2 cloves garlic, minced
- 2 cups beef stock or game stock (see recipe)
- 2 cups crushed tomatoes and juice
- 2 cups hot salsa
- 2 tsp. chili powder
- 1 tsp. black pepper
- 1/2 cup honey
- 1 tsp. salt
- 1 jalapeño pepper, diced 1/4"

SERVES: 4 to 6

GAME PILAF

In a Dutch oven, heat butter to a fast bubble. Add game cubes and brown. Add onions, carrots and celery. Sauté for 2 to 3 minutes stirring often to keep from sticking. Add red peppers, mushrooms, and rice. Sauté for 2 minutes. Add bay leaves, black pepper, Worcestershire sauce and game or beef stock. Stir to combine. Cut parchment paper into a circle the size of a pan top. Brush paper with butter to keep if from sticking to cooked rice. Place paper on top of rice mixture and bake for 1 hour in a 350° oven.

When rice is tender, remove from oven. Remove paper top and bay leaves. Toss rice mixture with a fork and serve.

Chef John's Tips

- The reason for the paper top is to let the liquid evaporate while baking. To make the paper circle, fold a square sheet of brown paper in half. Then fold in half again. Next, lay the folded paper on a flat surface. Fold the paper in half to make a V or funnel-shape. Repeat one more time. Hold folded paper over Dutch oven, placing the point in the center of the dish. Mark the side and cut open the paper and it should (with some luck) fit the opening. Brush with butter.
- Do not cover rice with a tight lid as you will make a watery, sticky mess!
- It is also important to brown the game first or you will have a bland, discolored dish.
- If you wish to use upland fowl, dice skinless pieces into 1/4" cubes and prepare the same as for ground game.

Game Pilaf Ingredients

- 1 Tbsp. butter
- 1 1/2 cups game, diced in 1/2" cubes
- 1/2 cup red onions, cut in 1/2" cubes
- 1/2 cup carrots, cut in 1/2" cubes
- 1/2 cup celery, cut in 1/4" cubes
- 1/2 cup red pepper, cut in 1/2" cubes
- 1 cup mushrooms, cut into 1/2" cubes
- 1 1/2 cups long grained rice
- 2 bay leaves
- 1/8 tsp. black pepper
- 1 tsp. Worcestershire sauce
- 2 cups game or beef stock (see recipe)

SERVES: 4 to 6

OLD-FASHIONED GAME POT ROAST

Remove bones, fat and silver skin from game and cut into 2" cubes. Heat oil to almost smoke hot. Roll cubes in flour and shake off excess flour thoroughly. Add to oil and brown on all sides. Remove to a Dutch oven.

To the skillet add garlic, onions, parsnips/carrots and cook until tender. Add flour and gently combine. Add to meat. Add nutmeg, pepper, beef base, beef stock and sherry. Combine well. Cover and bake at 300° for 2 hours. Add mushrooms, tomato paste and gently combine. Return cover and bake for an additional 30 minutes.

Chef John's Tips

- I finish this with baking powder dumplings.
- If using dumplings, add 1 extra cup of beef stock.
- This dish goes well with literally everything.
- If you use a bone-in roast, the roast should be about 4 pounds.

Old Fashioned Game Pot Roast Ingredients

- 2 to 3 lbs. boneless game meat, cut into 2" cubes
- 1/4 cup olive oil
- 1/2 cup flour
- 2 cloves garlic, minced fine
- 2 cups onions, cubed 1"
- 1 1/2 cups parsnips or carrots, cut into 1/4" slices
- 1/2 tsp. nutmeg
- 1 tsp. black pepper
- 1 Tbsp. beef base
- 2 cups beef stock (see recipe)
- 1 cup dry sherry
- 2 cups fresh mushrooms, cut in 1/4" slices
- 2 Tbsp. tomato paste

SERVES: 4

GRILLED GAME BURGERS

In one small bowl, combine mayonnaise, German mustard and garlic to make a sauce. In another bowl, combine ground game, ground pork, onion salt and black pepper.

Form meat into 4 large flat patties, about 1" thick. Grill or pan-fry on medium heat. When brown on both sides, top each with 1 tablespoon barbecue sauce. Cook medium to medium well. Top each with one slice Swiss cheese and let it melt.

To serve, split bun. On top half place 2 tablespoons mayonnaise sauce, red pepper ring and 1/2 cup fried onions. Place burger patty on bottom half and serve with a kosher pickle spear.

Chef John's Tips

- Before grinding wild game, remove as much fat and silver skin as possible as this is where the unwanted strong flavors come from.
- The reason for adding ground pork to game is to impart extra flavor. If you are not a fat lover, add ground beef that is 75% lean, 25% fat.
- Do not turn patty often as turning causes them to dry out.
- Never press patty while cooking as that pushes out all the juices and flavors. Remember - I may be watching!

Grilled Game Burgers Ingredients

- 1/2 cup mayonnaise
- 1/4 cup German mustard
- 2 small cloves garlic, minced
- 1 lb. ground game meat
- 1 lb. ground pork
- 1 tsp. onion salt
- 1 tsp. freshly ground black pepper
- 1/2 cup barbecue sauce
- 4 slices Swiss cheese
- 4 large hamburger buns
- 1 red pepper, cut into 8 slices
- 2 cups fried onions

MAKES 4 BURGERS

Game Bacon Lettuce Tomato Sandwich

Remove all fat and silver skin from steaks. Grill to desired doneness. Toast bread. Spread one side of each slice with a generous amount of tartar sauce. Top one slice with lettuce, 3 slices tomato and 3 strips bacon. Slice steak as thin as you can and add to sandwich. Top with other toast. Cut in half and serve with horseradish and dill pickle.

Chef John's Tips

- I sometimes make my sandwiches by splitting French bread in half, brushing it with olive oil and grilling the bread open faced.
- This is also great with boneless breast of pheasant or leftover game roast. To heat roast slices, sauté quickly in hot oil.

Game Bacon Lettuce Tomato Sandwich Ingredients

- *4 steaks, 1" thick*
- *8 slices hard crusted bread*
- *1/2 cup tartar sauce*
- *4 lettuce leaves*
- *12 slices tomatoes, 1/3" thick*
- *12 strips bacon, cooked crisp (fat drained off)*
- *Salt and pepper to taste*

MAKES 4 SANDWICHES

GAME HASH

Boil and cool potatoes. Dice into 1/4" cubes.

Remove fat and silver skin from game meat. Cut into 1/4" cubes. Heat oil almost smoke hot. Add meat and brown. Add garlic, onions, salt, pepper and cook until onions are tender. Add chili sauce, barbecue sauce and dill pickles. Bring to a boil. Let simmer 2 minutes. Add potatoes. Reduce heat to low and cook until potatoes are hot. Very gently combine and serve.

Chef John's Tips

- I like mine with poached eggs and rye toast.
- Any red game meat will taste great.

Game Hash Ingredients

- 2 cups red potatoes, boiled with skins on

- 1 1/2 cups game meat, cut in 1/4" cubes

- 1 Tbsp. olive oil or butter

- 1 clove garlic, minced fine

- 1 cup red onions, diced 1/4"

- 1 tsp. salt

- 1/2 tsp. black pepper

- 1 cup chili sauce

- 1/2 cup barbecue sauce

- 1/2 cup dill pickles, diced 1/4"

SERVES: 4

GAME PORCUPINE MEATBALLS

In a large bowl, combine game, pork, rice, onions, red wine, salt, pepper and chili powder.

Shape into 1 1/2" meatballs making sure they are pressed firm. Heat oil in a skillet and brown meatballs. Gently place meatballs in a casserole dish.

Combine beef stock, spaghetti sauce, Worcestershire sauce and Tabasco sauce and place on top of the meatballs. Cover dish and bake at 350° for 1 hour. Test for doneness. When rice is tender and meat is cooked, remove and serve with Italian breadsticks or fresh bread to dip in the sauce.

Chef John's Tips

- This is an excellent appetizer. Of course, it works very well as an entree or in a submarine roll as a sandwich.

Game Porcupine Meatballs Ingredients

- 1 lb. ground game

- 1/2 lb. ground pork

- 2/3 cup uncooked long grained rice

-1/2 cup onions, diced 1/4"

- 1/2 cup red wine

- 1 1/2 tsp. garlic salt

- 1 tsp. black pepper, freshly ground

- 1 tsp. chili powder

- 1 Tbsp. vegetable oil

- 1 cup beef stock (see recipe)

- 2 cups plain spaghetti sauce

- 2 tsp. Worcestershire sauce

- 3 drops Tabasco sauce

SERVES: 4 to 6

GAME GOULASH

Goulash soup is one of the great staples of Central Europe. It is also one of the heartiest and most delicious soups ever created.

Place olive oil in a heavy soup pot and heat almost until smoke hot. Roll cubed meat in flour and shake off excess flour. Add to oil. Add salt, pepper and brown mixing with a wooden spoon. Remove meat and set aside.

Add garlic, onions, celery and sauté stirring until vegetables are transparent. Add remaining flour and stir while cooking for two minutes. Add cooked meat and paprika and stir. Add beef stock, tomatoes and juice, tomato purée, and simmer slowly for 1 1/2 hours.

Add mushrooms, potatoes, Worcestershire sauce and simmer until potatoes are tender, but not mushy (about 30 minutes). Adjust seasoning with salt and pepper. If soup is too thick, add more beef stock to desired consistency. Serve with a dollop of sour cream.

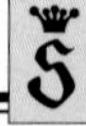

Chef John's Tips

- If you are a pepper lover, add 8 ounces of red bell peppers diced 1/2". Cook with mushrooms and potatoes.

Game Goulash Ingredients

- *1/4 cup olive oil*
- *1 1/2 lbs. game meat, very lean, cubed 1"*
- *1/2 cup flour*
- *1 tsp. salt*
- *1 tsp. coarse ground black pepper*
- *3 mashed garlic cloves*
- *3 cups onions, diced 1/2"*
- *3 cups celery, peeled and diced 1/2"*
- *2 tsp. Hungarian paprika*
- *1 quart beef stock (see recipe)*
- *6 cups diced tomatoes and juice*
- *2 cups tomato purée*
- *3 cups fresh mushrooms, sliced 1/4"*
- *2 cups potatoes, diced 1/2"*
- *1 Tbsp. Worcestershire sauce*
- *sour cream for topping*

SERVES: 6-8

BROWN BEER CRUMBLED BURGER

Heat a large heavy skillet. Add ground pork, ground game and garlic. Cook until it just starts to brown. It will look gray. Add onions, celery, mushrooms and spices. Stir well with a wooden spoon. Cook for 3 minutes. Stir in beer. Simmer on low heat for 20 minutes. Serve on toasted buns with yellow mustard and ketchup.

Chef John's Tips

- This is almost like sloppy Joe mix. If you wish, you can use barbecue sauce instead of beer.
- This is excellent over corn bread.
- If you wish, add 2 small hot peppers of your choice, sliced thin. Remove the seeds and stem.

Brown Beer Crumbled Burger Ingredients

- 1 lb. ground pork
- 1 lb. ground game
- 2 cloves garlic, minced fine
- 1 cup onion, diced 1/2"
- 1 cup celery, sliced 1/4"
- 1 cup mushrooms, sliced 1/4"
- 2 tsp. salt
- 1 tsp. black pepper
- 1 tsp. ground cumin
- 1/2 tsp. ground coriander
- 1 tsp. fennel seeds
- 1/2 cup dark beer
- 4 to 6 buns

SERVES: 4 to 6

GAME SCALLOPPINE

From a boneless roast, remove fat and silver skin. Slice into 1/2" thick slices across the grain. Flatten slices to 1/4" thick in a plastic bag with a broad meat mallet. Dredge venison in flour. Shake off excess flour. Set aside.

Combine parsley flakes, lemon zest and freshly ground black pepper in a bowl.

In a large sauté pan, heat butter to a fast bubble. Add shallots and garlic. Top with venison slices. Sauté on medium heat until brown on bottom. Turn venison and stir shallots. Sauté until bottom is brown. Add wine and tarragon. Let simmer for two minutes. Remove meat to a heated serving platter. Sprinkle parsley fleck mixture over scallops. Top with vegetable sauce from pan and serve with pasta, egg noodles or spätzles.

Chef John's Tips

- The best meat to use is loin tenderloins.
- Elk and antelope are also delicious this way.

Game Scalloppine Ingredients

- 8 slices venison, 3 oz. each
- 1/2 cup seasoned flour (see recipe)
- 2 tsp. fresh parsley, minced, no stems
- 1 tsp. lemon zest
- 1/2 tsp. freshly ground black pepper
- 1 Tbsp. clarified butter (see recipe)
- 2 Tbsp. shallots, diced fine
- 1 clove garlic, minced fine
- 1/2 cup dry white wine
- 2 tsp. fresh tarragon, minced

SERVES: 4

GAME CUTLETS

Beat eggs for egg wash and set aside.

Remove all fat, sinews and silver skin from meat. Cut game meat into slices 1/2" thick. Flatten to 1/4" thickness in a plastic bag with a meat mallet. Do not over pound and tear the meat.

Dredge slices in seasoned flour. Dip in egg wash and then in bread crumbs. Shake off excess crumbs. Heat clarified butter in a large sauté pan. When butter starts to bubble, add game slices and brown. Turn slices over and splash with lemon juice. Cover and put into 350° oven for about 15 minutes. Place three schnitzels on each plate and garnish each schnitzel with a lemon slice.

Chef John's Tips

- Schnitzels should be free from all fat and connective tissue. They should be sliced thin and shaped in an oval or triangle.
- For game schnitzels, garnish with hot, fresh orange cranberry sauce.
- Don't take a short cut on the bread crumbs. Make them fresh. You will taste the difference.

VARIATIONS:
Schnitzel Holstein: Place two fried eggs sunny-side up, two strips of anchovies and twelve capers on top of schnitzels before serving.
Schnitzel Hunters-style: Cook schnitzels per recipe above and cover with mushroom sauce.
Schnitzel Italian style: Finish cutlets by topping with tomato sauce and provolone cheese.
Caper Schnitzel: Serve with 1/4 cup of caper sauce over each portion.

Game Cutlets Ingredients

- *1 lb. game meat, sliced into 1/2" slices*
- *1 cup seasoned flour (see recipe)*
- *1 cup egg wash (see recipe)*
- *3 cups fresh white bread crumbs (see recipe)*
- *1/4 cup clarified butter (see recipe)*
- *2 Tbsp. fresh lemon juice*
- *12 lemon slices*

SERVES: 4

CHEF JOHN'S GAME SAUERBRATEN

Put all marinade ingredients into a large container and stir well. Remove all fat and silver skin from game meat. Pierce meat at random with boning knife. Add meat to marinade, making sure meat is completely covered with liquid. Place in a covered container in the refrigerator and marinate for 72 hours. (If you marinate for less than 72 hours, game will be tough. If you marinate for more than 72 hours, the meat will become dry and flavorless.)

Remove meat, wipe dry with towel, and brown in hot oil in a frying pan or skillet. Remove to a large pot or brazier. Place marinade in with the meat. Cover, bring to a boil, and simmer for 2 1/2 hours or until tender. When meat is done, transfer to dry pan. Cover with a damp cloth and keep warm.

Remove bay leaves. Purée liquid and vegetables in a blender. Place in a heavy pot, whip crushed ginger snap cookies into liquid, stirring until smooth. Add raisins. Simmer for five minutes. Hold for service. Cut meat across the grain and serve with a two-ounce ladle of sauce per portion.

Chef John's Tips

- Boneless roast works best.
- There is extra sauce for leftovers

Chef John's Game Sauerbraten Ingredients

MARINADE:

- 2 cups cold beef stock (see recipe)
- 1 Tbsp. beef base
- 1 1/2 cups red wine vinegar
- 2 cups Burgundy wine
- 1 cup thinly sliced onions
- 1/2 cup thinly sliced carrots
- 1/2 cup thinly sliced celery
- 2 cups diced tomato pieces and liquid
- 2 Tbsp. brown sugar
- 2 cloves chopped garlic
- 1 tsp. salt
- 2 bay leaves
- 6 crushed black peppercorns
- 4 whole cloves
- 1 Tbsp. juniper berries

GAME MEAT:

- 4 lbs. game roast (game of choice)
- 1/3 cup vegetable oil
- 1 1/2 cups crushed ginger snap cookies
- 2/3 cup raisins

SERVES: 4 to 6

GAME BURGUNDY with FRESH MUSHROOMS

Remove all fat and silver skin from meat. Cut into cubes. Roll cubes in flour.

In a Dutch oven, heat olive oil. Add game cubes and cook until game is brown on all sides. Stir with a wooden spoon to keep from sticking to bottom. Add remaining flour and combine well. Add onions, garlic, carrots, beef stock, beef base, wine, thyme, brown sugar, tomato paste and black pepper. Cover and bake for 1 1/2 hours at 350°. Add mushrooms and bake for 30 minutes.

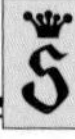

Chef John's Tips

- This is one of those traditional recipes. It works well with all red game meat.
- Be sure to use a good quality Burgundy wine.

Game Burgundy with Fresh Mushrooms Ingredients

- 2 lbs. game, cubed 1/2"

- 1 cup seasoned flour (see recipe)

- 1/4 cup olive oil

- 2 cups onions, cut 1/2" cubes

- 3 cloves garlic, minced fine

- 1 1/2 cups carrots, cut in 1/4" cubes

- 1 cup beef stock (see recipe)

- 2 tsp. beef base

- 1 quart Burgundy wine

- 1 tsp. thyme

- 1 Tbsp. brown sugar

- 1/2 cup tomato paste

- 1/2 tsp. black pepper

- 2 cups fresh mushrooms, cut in quarters

GAME ONION-HORSERADISH MEATLOAF

In a large bowl, beat eggs. Add chili sauce, horseradish, pepper, garlic salt, Worcestershire sauce and rolled oats. Combine well. Add onions and meat and combine the mixture well. Place mixture into a loaf pan. Bake at 375° for 1 hour. Test for doneness. Temperature on inside should be 165° or there should be no red color to the meat. Let rest for 5 minutes. Cut and serve.

Chef John's Tips

- A slice of cold meatloaf with cheese makes a great sandwich.

Game Onion-Horseradish Meatloaf Ingredients

- 2 eggs, whipped
- 1/4 cup chili sauce
- 1/4 cup horseradish, pressed dry
- 1 tsp. black pepper
- 2 tsp. garlic salt
- 1 Tbsp. Worcestershire sauce
- 1/4 cup old fashioned rolled oats
- 1 cup onions, diced 1/4"
- 1 1/2 lbs. ground game
- 1/2 lb. ground beef

SERVES: 4 to 6

QUICK and EASY GAME STIR FRY

Remove all bones, fat and silver skin from meat. Cut into pieces the size of your small finger.

Cut all vegetables to size and measure out all liquid. Combine cornstarch with beef stock.

In a large non-stick skillet, heat oil almost smoke hot. Add game and brown on all sides. Remove meat, leaving oil. Place in covered bowl. Add onions, celery, carrots and sauté until onions and celery are clear. Add pea pods, green onions, ginger, soy sauce and browned meat. Simmer for 2 minutes. Add cornstarch/beef stock mixture and mix well. Simmer on medium heat until slightly thickened and liquid is clear.

Chef John's Tips

- This works well with all game and fowl. I also toss in some shrimp just for fun.
- Serve with white rice or wild rice. This also hits the spot over baked potatoes.
- This is a great dish to do over a hot campfire in a heavy black skillet.

Quick and Easy Game Stir Fry Ingredients

- 1 1/2 lbs. game meat, cut 3" long, 1/2" wide, 1/2" thick
- 1 Tbsp. cornstarch
- 1/2 cup beef stock (see recipe)
- 1 Tbsp. vegetable oil
- 1 cup onions, sliced in 1/4" strips
- 1 cup celery, peeled and sliced in 1/4" slices
- 1 cup carrots, sliced in 1/4" slices on the bias
- 1 cup snow pea pods, fresh or frozen
- 1/2 cup green onions, 1/4" slices
- 1 Tbsp. fresh ginger, diced 1/4"
- 1/4 cup soy sauce

SERVES: 4 to 6

GAME DINNER in a PAN

Remove all fat and silver skin from steaks. Peel carrots and cut in half the long way. Cut each half in 2 pieces to make 8 carrot quarters.

Wash squash and trim off end. Cut the same as carrots. Wash mushrooms and leave whole. Peel onions and slice into halves.

On a hot fire or burner place a thick skillet. (I use cast iron or steel.) Add oil and heat smoke hot. Add onions and brown on both sides. Remove onions to a plate. Add carrots and fry to a golden brown on both sides. Add to the onions on plate. If needed, add more oil. Return oil to smoke hot and cook squash the same as carrots. Add to vegetable plate. Return pan to hot. Add steaks and brown well on both sides. Add mushrooms, red peppers, salt, pepper, Worcestershire sauce and basil. With a wooden spoon remove all crust from the bottom of the pan leaving it in the pan for flavor. Add vegetables back to pan. First add onions, then carrots and squash. Remove pan to cool side of fire or turn burner to low.

Cover with tortilla shell. Cook for 5 minutes. Remove tortilla shells to 4 plates. Top each tortilla shell with a steak, onion slice, 2 pieces carrot, 2 pieces squash, one mushroom and pour liquid evenly over the top of the vegetables.

Chef John's Tips

- A large thick pan is essential. A lightweight pan will burn all ingredients before they cook.
- Duck, geese and pheasant breast are also excellent cooked this way. Cook half a breast slab as if it was a steak. To serve, cut slabs on the bias into thin slices.

Ingredients

- 6 - 8 oz. game steaks
- 2 carrots, 1/4" thick slices
- 2 summer squash, green or yellow
- 4 large fresh mushrooms
- 2 onions, medium size, 1/4" thick slices
- 1/3 cup olive oil
- 2 red peppers
- 1/2 tsp. salt
- 1/4 tsp. black pepper
- 1 Tbsp. Worcestershire sauce
- 1 Tbsp. dry basil
- 4 large tortilla shells

SERVES: 4

BOILED GAME DINNER

Remove all fat and silver skin from roast.

Heat oil in a sauté pan to almost smoke hot. Add meat and brown on all sides. Remove meat to a pot. Add water, garlic, caraway seeds, bay leaves, beef base, salt and pepper. Boil slowly with meat for 2 3/4 hours. Skim off foam from time to time.

Add vegetables, including potatoes and simmer until tender (approximately 1/2 hour). Remove meat and vegetables and serve with horseradish sauce or hot German mustard.

Chef John's Tips

- I love this recipe cooked over a campfire in a large Dutch oven.
- Serve horseradish and cider vinegar with dinner.

Ingredients

- 1/3 cup vegetable oil

- 3 to 4 lbs. game roast

- 3 quarts water

- 3 cloves garlic

- 2 tsp. caraway seeds

- 3 bay leaves

- 1 Tbsp. beef base

- 2 tsp. salt

- 1 tsp. cracked black pepper

- 2 cups onions, diced 1"

- 2 cups carrots, sliced 1/2"

- 2 cups celery, peeled and sliced 2" long

- 1 head cabbage, cut into 8 wedges

- 4 medium red potatoes, unpeeled

SERVES: 4 to 6

GAME CHOPS with GREEN CHILI POCKETS

This recipe has three steps.

To make rub. Remove all excess fat and silver skin from meat. To prepare steaks cut a deep horizontal pocket in each steak. Leave 1/2 inch on the sides and end. Combine black pepper, Cajun seasoning and garlic powder. Rub on steak and place steak in plastic bag with olive oil overnight.

To make stuffing: Heat olive oil. Add onions and sauté until tender. Add green chilies and spices and simmer for 5 minutes on low. Add bread crumbs and combine well to make thick vegetable paste.

To cook: Stuff steaks with 2 tablespoons chili stuffing. Spray outside of steak with olive oil and grill to medium rare.

Chef John's Tips

- If you like hot, add hot peppers of your choice.

Game Chops with Green Chili Pockets Ingredients

- 4 game steaks (8 -10 ounces each)

Rub:

- 1 Tbsp. black pepper

- 1 Tbsp. Cajun seasoning

- 1/2 tsp. garlic powder

- 2 tsp. olive oil

Stuffing:

- 2 Tbsp. olive oil

- 1 cup onions, diced 1/4"

- 1 cup canned green chilies

- 1 tsp. dry oregano

- 1 tsp. basil

- 3/4 cup bread crumbs (see recipe)

SERVES: 4

GAME LIVER with BACON RASPBERRY VINAIGRETTE

Remove all skin and veins from liver. This is very important. Slice and soak overnight in milk. In a skillet, cook bacon on medium heat. Add onions and peppers and cook until tender. Combine vinegar, beef base and add to vegetables. Bring to a boil and reduce heat. Simmer for 3 minutes.

Remove liver from milk. Pat dry with paper towels. Heat olive oil to almost smoke hot. Dredge slices in flour. Shake off excess. Add to olive oil and brown on both sides. Add onions and bacon base. Bring to a boil and serve.

Chef John's Tips

- You can prepare liver from fowl the same way.
- If you can't find raspberry vinegar, red wine vinegar works equally well.
- The milk does not make the liver tender. It draws out the excess blood.
- I like my liver cooked medium rare.

Game Liver with Bacon Raspberry Vinaigrette Ingredients

- 8 game livers, sliced 1/2" thick
- 2 cups milk
- 6 pieces bacon, diced 1/2"
- 1 cup onions, 1/4" slices
- 1 cup red peppers, 1/4" slices
- 1/4 cup raspberry vinegar
- 1 tsp. beef base
- 1/4 cup olive oil
- 1 cup seasoned flour (see recipe)

SERVES: 4

COCONUT GAME CURRY

Trim all fat, silver skin and sinews from meat. Cut into cubes. Dredge in flour. Shake off excess flour. In a Dutch oven, heat oil almost smoke hot. Add antelope cubes. Brown well on all sides. Remove meat to a plate. Add garlic and onions and cook until tender. Add coconut milk, curry powder, mushroom soup, beef stock, beef base, dry mustard, black pepper, jalapeño peppers and combine well. Add cooked meat. Cover and bake at 350° for 2 hours.

Place nuts and coconut in a bowl. Toss with honey to coat well. Place on a well buttered sheet pan. Spread out evenly into a thin layer. Add to 350° oven and bake for 20 minutes or until golden brown. Remove from oven. Let cool on pan.

Remove antelope after 2 hours cooking time. Serve over white rice topped with honey coconut cashew pieces.

Chef John's Tips

- By all means serve with your favorite chutney.
- This is an excellent way to prepare game with a strong wild taste.
- I line my sheet pan with foil for roasting nuts or coconut as it is much easier to clean.
- If you can't find coconut milk, use coconut pina colada mix.
- Yes, I call for mushroom soup. It helps save time and has a consistent flavor.

Coconut Game Curry
Ingredients

- 1 lb. antelope, cubed in 1" squares
- 1/2 cup seasoned flour (see recipe)
- 2 Tbsp. olive oil
- 2 cloves minced garlic
- 1 cup onions, sliced 1/4"
- 1 cup coconut milk
- 3 tsp. curry powder
  (see recipe)
- 1 can mushroom soup
- 1 cup beef stock (see recipe)
- 1 Tbsp. beef base
- 1 tsp. dry mustard
- 1 tsp. freshly ground black pepper
- 2 small jalapeño peppers, minced with seeds

TOPPING

- 1/2 cup cashew pieces
- 1/2 cup shredded coconut
- 1 Tbsp. honey

SERVES: 4

CAMP GAME VEGETABLE and BARLEY SOUP

Remove all fat and silver skin from meat. In a Dutch oven place oil and heat to almost smoke hot. Add meat and brown well on all sides. Remove to a clean plate.

Add cubed vegetables except cabbage and sauté until onions are clear, stirring often to keep from burning. Add pearl barley and combine well. Cook for 1 minute. Add browned game roast, cabbage, spices, ketchup, Worcestershire sauce and water. Cover and cook over medium heat for about 1 1/2 to 2 hours. When meat is tender, soup is ready. Adjust seasoning and serve.

Chef John's Tips

- It is important to use as heavy a covered pot as is available. I realize light weight gear is important for back packing and portages.
- If using a thin or light pot to make the soup, be sure to cook over low heat for longer periods of time and stir often with a non-metal spoon to keep barley from burning on the bottom of the pot.
- Do not worry if not all the ingredients are available. Just use what you have.
- Make sure to brown the roast, for additional flavor.
- My Mother makes this soup every Saturday on the farm. She has since the 1950's and still does today. She adds Baking Powder Dumplings the last 10 minutes of cooking.
- Be sure to add liquid. As the soup cooks, the barley will absorb a lot of liquid. Keep a close eye on the liquid.

Camp Game Vegetable and Barley Soup Ingredients

- 3 to 4 lbs. game roast (boneless or bone-in)
- 1/2 cup oil
- 2 cups onions, cut in 1" cubes
- 2 cups carrots, cut in 1" cubes
- 1 cup celery, cut in 1" cubes
- 4 tomatoes, stems removed, cut in 1" cubes
- 1 1/2 cups pearl barley
- 1 small head cabbage, cut in 1" cubes
- 3 bay leaves
- 1 tsp. black pepper
- 2 tsp. thyme
- 1 1/2 cups ketchup
- 1/4 cup Worcestershire sauce
- 1 gallon water

SERVES: 6 to 8

GAME CHILI

In a Dutch oven, heat oil hot. Add minced garlic, onions, celery, meat and cook until meat is brown. Add all ingredients except kidney beans and cover. Bake in a 350° oven for 1 1/2 hours. Add kidney beans, salt and pepper. Combine and bake one hour. Adjust chili powder or red pepper flakes to taste.

Chef John's Tips

- This recipe is not going to be a thick chili.
- You may also add chili beans.
- Garnish with sour cream and shredded Swiss cheese or a few crushed cashews on top.
- For Texas style, add jalapeño peppers that have been deseeded and diced.

Game Chili Ingredients

- *1 Tbsp. olive oil*
- *2 cloves garlic, minced*
- *3 cups onions, diced 1/2"*
- *2 cups celery, sliced 1/4"*
- *2 lbs. ground game*
- *3 cups diced tomatoes and juice*
- *1 cup tomato sauce*
- *1 Tbsp. beef base (level)*
- *1 Tbsp. chili powder*
- *1/2 tsp. ground cumin*
- *1 tsp. black pepper*
- *1/4 tsp. cinnamon*
- *1 cup red wine*
- *1 Tbsp. Worcestershire sauce*
- *1 tsp. red pepper flakes*
- *3 cups kidney beans, drained*
- *1 tsp. salt*
- *1/2 tsp. black pepper*

SERVES: 6 to 8

KICK YOUR BUTT BURGERS

In a skillet, melt butter and sauté onions and garlic until onions are tender (about 2 minutes on medium heat). Remove onions, garlic and butter to a bowl. Place in refrigerator to cool. When onion mixture is cool, add ground game and beef, spices and bread crumbs. Combine well by hand.

Shape into 4 to 6 patties. Grill to medium doneness over medium heat or fry in a heavy skillet.

Chef John's Tips

- The heat comes from the cayenne pepper. Be careful not to add too much.
- If you are in camp and have no fresh bread crumbs, don't cry. Simply dice slices of bread as fine as you can.
- Make sure to cook burgers until medium doneness.
- For another flavor, substitute ground pork for ground beef.

Kick Your Butt Burgers Ingredients

- 1/4 cup butter
- 1/2 cup red onions, diced 1/4" cubes
- 2 cloves garlic, diced 1/4" cubes
- 1 1/2 lbs. ground game
- 1 lb. ground beef
- 1 tsp. salt
- 1 tsp. black pepper
- 1/2 tsp. rub sage
- 1/4 tsp. cayenne pepper
- 1/4 tsp. celery seeds
- 1/2 tsp. allspice
- 2/3 cup fresh bread crumbs (see recipe)

SERVES: 4 to 6

AFTER the HUNT GAME SAUTÉ

Remove fat and silver skin from game. Slice into 1/2" thick pieces and flatten with a mallet. Dredge in seasoned flour. Heat butter until it is almost smoke hot. Add venison slices and sauté until cooked. In a separate frying pan, sauté onions for one minute. Drain off butter. Add white wine, sherry and salt. Cover and simmer for two minutes. Add chopped parsley and toss to combine.

Place three slices of game on a hot plate and top with onion and onion liquid.

Chef John's Tips

- This recipe works well with all red game meat, including bear, antelope, elk and boar.
- If wine is not available, 1/4 cup of brandy or rum works well.
- Chopped Parsley adds color. If not available, "Don't Worry About It".

After the Hunt Game Sauté Ingredients

- *1 1/2 lbs. game, cut into twelve 1/2" slices*
- *1 cup seasoned flour (see recipe)*
- *1/4 cup clarified butter (see recipe)*
- *6 cups onions sliced 1/4"*
- *1/4 cup white wine*
- *1/4 cup dry sherry*
- *pinch of salt*
- *2 Tbsp. parsley flakes*

SERVES: 4

Upland Game Recipes

PHEASANT HIPS STROGANOFF

Remove skin, bones and sinews from thighs and dice as fine as you can. In a bowl, place pork, ground pheasant, parsley, rye bread crumbs, tarragon, onion powder, salt, black pepper and beaten egg. Combine well and make meatballs the size of walnuts.

In a large skillet heat olive oil. Add meatballs and brown on all sides on medium heat. Add mushrooms. Cover and cook 2 minutes on low heat. In a bowl, whisk smooth the mushroom soup, Half and Half, sherry and sour cream. Add to meatballs. Simmer for 10 minutes and serve with pasta, wild rice or white rice.

Chef John's Tips

- Of course, this works well with both white and dark meat. But this is a great way to use up the dark meat.
- Do not try to use leg meat as it has too many sinews and tendons.
- White bread crumbs work if you don't have rye bread crumbs.
- If you have a grinder, grind pheasant thigh instead of dicing it.
- If you don't want to use pork, add 1/2 cup soft cream cheese and ground beef.
- Always check birds for shot.

Pheasant Hips Stroganoff Ingredients

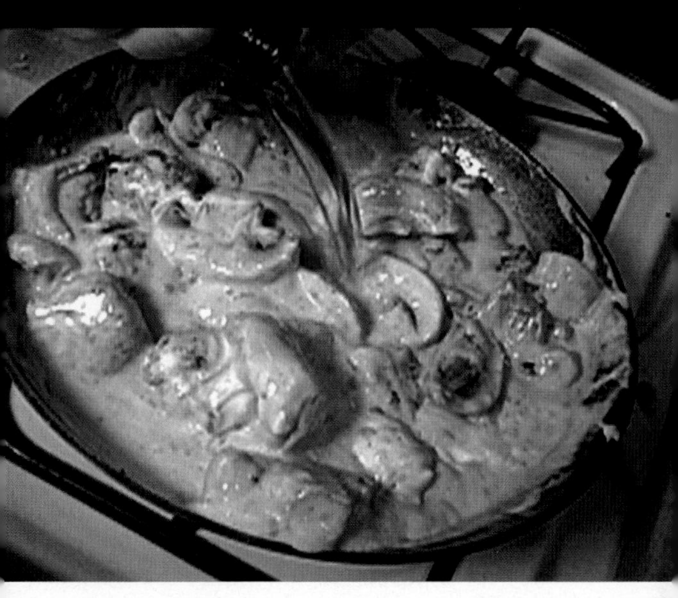

- 3 cups boneless pheasant thigh meat, diced fine
- 2 cups ground pork
- 1 Tbsp. parsley
- 1 cup fresh rye bread crumbs (see recipe)
- 1/2 tsp. tarragon
- 1/2 tsp. onion powder
- 1 tsp. salt
- 1 tsp. black pepper, freshly ground
- 1 egg, beaten slightly
- 1 Tbsp. olive oil
- 1 cup fresh mushrooms, cut into quarters
- 2 cans Cream of Mushroom soup
- 8 oz. Half and Half
- 1/4 cup sherry
- 1/2 cup sour cream

SERVES: 4

TEN STEPS to a PERFECT ROAST TURKEY

1. If turkey is frozen, thaw in the refrigerator 24 to 72 hours.

2. Remove neck from body cavity and giblets from neck cavity. Cut wings off at first joint.

3. Cook neck, giblets (except for liver as it is too bitter) and wings in a pan with 2 cups onions, 1 cup celery, 2 bay leaves, 1 teaspoon thyme, 1/2 teaspoon black pepper and 2 quarts cold water. Cook until meat is tender.

   - Remove meat from neck bone

   - Save stock and diced meat and giblets to be used in your favorite dressing recipe.

   - Never stuff your bird. Cook stuffing in a covered baking dish.

4. Rinse turkey inside and out with cold water. Place salt and white pepper in the cavity.

5. Place one large or two medium peeled onions in the cavity.

6. Rub the skin lightly with vegetable oil.

7. Place turkey in a roaster bag and bake as directed.

8. Roast at 225° F.

9. Check for doneness after 2 hours of roasting. Turkey is fully cooked when the thigh's internal temperature is 180° F. The thickest part of the breast should read 170°.

10. When done, let the turkey stand for 10 to 15 minutes before carving.

Ten Steps to a Perfect Roast Turkey

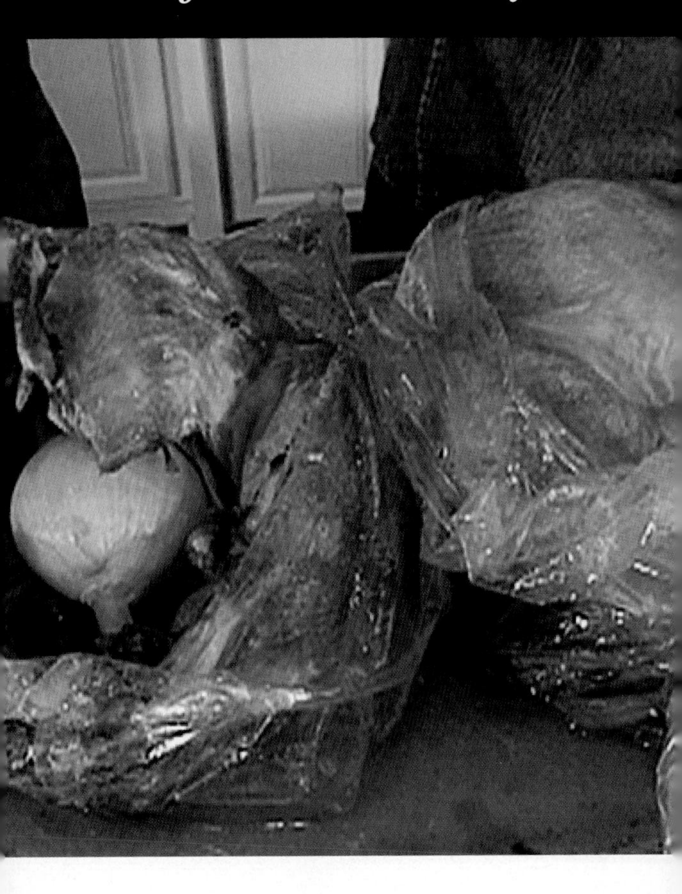

Chef John's Tips

- Correctly roasting wild turkey is one of the most difficult entrees to prepare in my opinion.

GRILLED WILD TURKEY

After skinning or picking turkey, wash and clean well. Set bird breast side up. Remove the two breast slabs by cutting next to the breast bone and removing the breasts in two large pieces. Remove the thigh and leg in one piece on each side. Lay thigh-leg on a cutting board, inside up. Cut off the leg at the first joint, leaving thigh. Remove the bone from the thigh. This will give you a good piece of dark meat. From the breast slabs remove all shiny silver skin and sinews.

Place turkey breast pieces and thigh pieces in a stainless steel bowl or glass dish. Top with onions, garlic, wine, lemon juice, bay leaves and herb dressing to make a marinade. Cover tightly and refrigerate for three days.

To grill, remove turkey pieces from bowl or dish, and place on grill. Baste often with marinade and grill until done. Be careful not to overcook.

Place cooked turkey pieces on a cutting board and slice thinly at an angle. Serve with Hollandaise or mushroom sauce or my personal favorite, Béarnaise sauce.

Chef John's Tips

- Since the turkey legs are not good for this recipe, save them for soup.
- You can also use this recipe with domestic turkey under 20 pounds.

Grilled Wild Turkey Ingredients

- 1 wild turkey
- 2 cups sliced onions
- 3 cloves garlic
- 1/2 cup dry white wine
- 1 Tbsp. fresh lemon juice
- 3 bay leaves
- 1 pint herb dressing

SERVES: 4

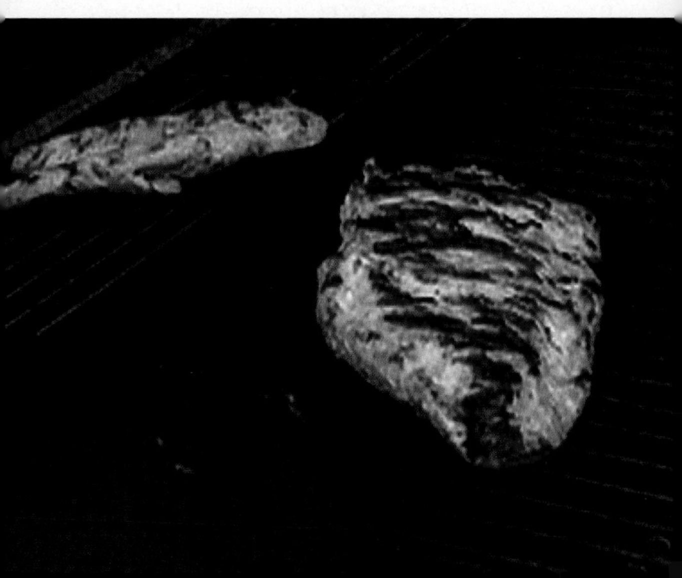

WILD TURKEY CHILI SOUP

Remove all skin, sinews and bones from turkey. Heat half the oil in a large heavy soup pot. Add turkey and brown. Remove turkey pieces to a dish to hold. Add remaining oil to soup pot. Heat. Add garlic, onions, red pepper and sauté until tender. Combine flour and cumin and add to vegetables. Cook for 1 minute on medium heat, stirring gently to keep from sticking.

Add turkey pieces, red wine, beef stock and chopped tomatoes and simmer on low heat for 30 minutes. Add beans and scallions. Combine gently and simmer for 15 minutes. Add salt, pepper and chili powder to desired taste. Serve with diced avocado, shredded pepper cheese or sour cream.

Chef John's Tips

- You can also use goose, duck, pheasant hips or sage hens.
- I use the thigh, wings and leg meat from the turkey. I save all my upland game parts for this.
- After browning meat and vegetables, chili can be cooked in a crock pot.
- You may use your favorite cheese for garnish.

Wild Turkey Chili Soup Ingredients

- 4 cups turkey, diced 1/4"
- 1/4 cup olive oil
- 1 clove garlic, minced fine
- 1/2 cup onions, cut 1/2"
- 1 cup red pepper, cut 1/2"
- 2 Tbsp. flour
- 1/2 tsp. ground cumin
- 1/4 cup red wine
- 3 cups beef stock (see recipe)
- 3 cups diced tomato and juice
- 2 cups chili beans
- 1 cup butter beans, drained
- 1/2 cup chopped scallions (1/4 pound)
- 1 tsp. salt
- 1 tsp. black pepper
- 2 Tbsp. chili powder
- 1 avocado, diced 1/2" cubes
- 1 cup pepper cheese, shredded
- 1 cup sour cream

SERVES: 8

PHEASANT NEST OMELETS

In a bowl, beat eggs, milk, salt, white pepper and Worchestershire sauce to a froth. Set aside.

Heat a large non-stick pan until hot. Add butter and cook to a golden brown. Add pheasant and broccoli pieces. Sauté until hot. Add egg mixture and cook just until egg starts to thicken. Scramble egg mixture. Place tomato pieces in center. Remove from heat. Cover 1 minute. Place on a large platter and serve with tomato salsa.

Chef John's Tips

- Fresh salsa can be used as a sidedish.
- If you wish, you may use your favorite cheese as an additional topping. If you are really wild, also add sour cream and fresh green onions.

Pheasant Nest Omelets
Ingredients

- 8 eggs
- 1/4 cup milk
- 1 tsp. salt
- 1 pinch white pepper
- 1 tsp. Worcestershire sauce
- 1 Tbsp. butter
- 2 cups cooked pheasant meat, diced in 1/4" cubes
- 2 cups cooked broccoli, diced in 1/2" cubes
- 1 cup fresh tomatoes, diced in 1/2" pieces
- tomato salsa

SERVES: 4

PHEASANT À LA CREME

Remove skin from pheasant and cut into quarters.

Dredge pheasant pheasant in flour and shake off excess flour. Brown in hot oil.

Place in a Dutch oven. Add minced shallots and chicken stock. Cover and bake in a 350° oven for 2 hours. Add cream, salt, sherry and white wine, and continue baking until pheasant is tender and sauce is thick (about 1 1/2 hours). Season to taste with salt and pepper.

Chef John's Tips

- The secret to cooking moist, tender pheasant is to cook it, covered in chicken stock, over moderate heat for a long period of time.
- Rabbit can also be prepared this way.
- You must use the heaviest cream available to get the sauce to thicken. Do not substitute milk for cream as milk will not thicken. Milk will make a curdled mess.
- This recipe is the one I grew up with. My mother still makes the best in the "universe."
- Always check birds for shot.

Pheasant À La Creme
Ingredients

- 2 pheasants, 3-3 1/2 lbs.,
cut in quarters

- 1 1/2 cups seasoned flour (see recipe)

- 1 cup vegetable oil

- 1/2 cup minced shallots

- 2 cups chicken stock (see recipe)

- 2 pints heavy whipping cream

- 1 tsp. salt

- 3 oz. cream sherry

- 3 oz. white wine

SERVES: 2

LEMON PHEASANT FINGERS

Remove skin and silver skin from pheasant breasts and slice each breast into six strips about the size of a forefinger. Combine eggs and Parmesan cheese and beat to a smooth consistency. Heat butter in a large sauté pan. Dredge pheasant fingers in flour, dip into egg batter, and roll in bread crumbs. Sauté in butter until golden brown. Splash with lemon juice. Season with lemon pepper, salt and pepper. Turn down heat and cook for 3 minutes turning meat over to keep from over-browning.

Chef John's Tips

- Serve the fingers with assorted sauces.
- Prepare whole skinless, boneless breast the same way only finish in a 350° oven for 20 minutes.

Lemon Pheasant Fingers
Ingredients

- 4 boneless, skinless pheasant breasts
- 8 eggs
- 3/4 cup Parmesan cheese
- 1/3 cup clarified butter (see recipe)
- 1 cup seasoned flour (see recipe)
- 2 cups bread crumbs (see recipe)
- 1 Tbsp. fresh lemon juice
- 2 tsp. lemon pepper seasoning
- Salt and pepper to taste

SERVES: 4

BARBECUED GROUSE BUNDLES

Clean birds and soak in salted water for 1 hour.

Dice onions and combine with salt, pepper and 1/2 cup barbecue sauce. Place equal amounts in cavity of each bird. Wrap 2 slices of ham around birds. Remove 4 large cabbage leaves and fold around birds to make a blanket. Place a bird in center of double thick aluminum foil sheet 1 foot square. Cover with 1/4 cup barbecue sauce and fold the foil around the birds to make a bundle. Close tightly on top.

Bake in a 375° oven for one hour. Open bundle and fold sides down. Return to oven and bake for 15 minutes to make a crust. Remove from oven and serve.

To serve, remove bacon and brush birds with barbecue sauce. Serve in cabbage leaves and pour liquid from tin foil pouch over birds.

Chef John's Tips

- You may also do this on the outside barbecue or by a camp fire. Be careful when you turn the bundles not to let the liquid pour out. It takes a shorter time to cook over a campfire. Check for doneness after 45 minutes.
- Pastrami can be used instead of ham for peppery flavor.
- Always check bird for shot.

Barbecued Grouse Bundles Ingredients

- 4 grouse or partridges
- 2 onions, diced 1/2"
- 1 tsp. salt
- 1 tsp. black pepper
- 1 1/2 cups barbecue sauce
- 8 thin ham slices
- 1 head red cabbage

SERVES: 4

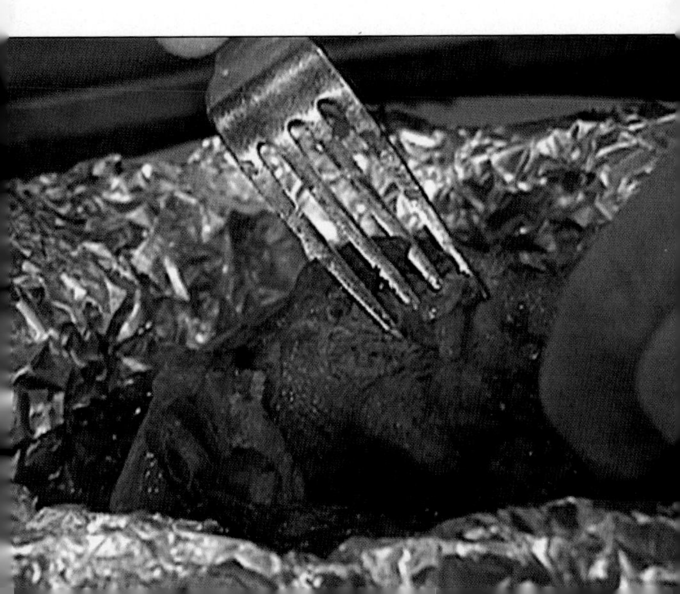

PHEASANT KATHLEEN SALAD

To prepare pheasant breast: Remove skin and bones from breast. Cut each whole breast into 8 strips the size of your little finger. Roll in flour. Shake off excess flour. Heat oil hot in a skillet and sauté fingers until done. Splash with Worcestershire sauce. Remove to a warm plate. Cover and hold. Assemble salad in advance.

To assemble salad plate: Chill 4 dinner plates. Wash strawberries and slice in 1/4 inch slices. Wash lettuce and shake dry. Crumble blue cheese in pearl sized pieces. Wash and pick leaves from parsley stems. Wash, peel and slice celery.

Arrange clockwise on a plate: a nest of lettuce, sliced strawberries, blueberry raisins, celery, 2 tomato wedges. Place cooked pheasant fingers in lettuce nest and serve with poppyseed dressing.

Garnish with freshly ground black pepper.

Chef John's Tips

- This works well with duck or goose breast. You may use lettuce of your choice.
- This salad is named for my wife, Kathleen, who is the love of my life.

Pheasant Kathleen Salad Ingredients

To prepare pheasant breast

- 2 whole pheasant breasts, cut into strips

- 1/2 cup seasoned flour (see recipe)

- 1 Tbsp. olive oil

- 1 tsp. Worcestershire sauce

To assemble salad plate

- 8 large fresh strawberries, cut in slices

- 2 heads leaf or bib lettuce

- 1 cup Stilton Blue Cheese

- 1/4 cup parsley

- 1 cup celery, peeled and cut in 1/4" slices

- 1 1/2 cups fresh blueberry raisins

- 2 tomatoes, cut into 6 wedges each

- poppyseed dressing (see recipe)

- freshly ground black pepper to taste

SERVES: 4

QUAIL HELENKA

This is an elegant and wonderful dish. It is named for my mother, who is the original inspiration for my cooking.

Wash quail and season cavities with salt and pepper. Stuff two blue prunes in each and wrap one bacon strip over the top. Wrap one bacon strip around each quail.

Bake in 375° oven for 40 minutes. Place one ounce brown sauce or gravy on small mound of dressing and place one quail on top. Repeat for other quail.

Chef John's Tips

- You may also use squab for this recipe.

Quail Helenka Ingredients

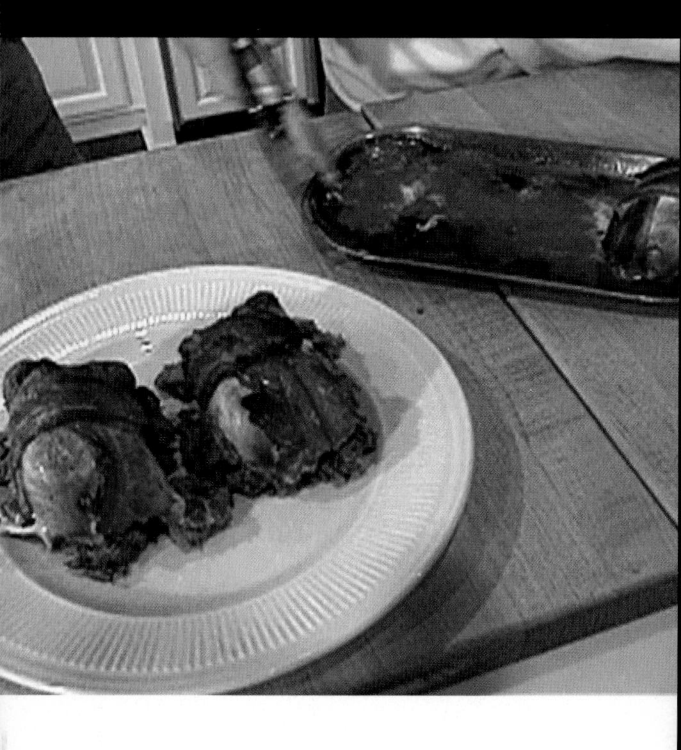

- *8 quail*
- *salt and pepper to taste*
- *16 blue prunes*
- *16 strips bacon*
- *4 cups brown sauce (see recipe)*
- *4 cups Hotel Stuffing (see recipe)*

SERVES: 4

Waterfowl Recipes

DUCK or GEESE in SAUERKRAUT

Clean and cut ducks into quarters. Remove wings. Trim off all excess fat and skin. Dredge in flour. Shake off excess flour. Heat oil in a Dutch oven. Add duck and brown well on all sides. Add onions and cook until tender. Add remaining flour and stir to combine. With a wooden spoon, stir crust off the bottom of pan. Add wine chicken stock, brown sugar, spices and chicken base.

Before you start to prepare ducks, rinse sauerkraut under cold water to remove salt. Strain well and gently add to duck base. Cover and bake at 350° for 2 hours. When ducks are tender, serve with dumplings, spätzle or boiled potatoes. A good German beer also tastes great!

Chef John's Tips

- You may use 1 large goose. If the goose is large, cut the breast into 4 pieces and separate the leg from the thigh. Two small geese are the same as one large goose.
- This recipe always tastes better the next day.
- Always check birds for shot.

Duck or Geese in Sauerkraut Ingredients

- 2 medium-sized ducks or 1 large goose

- 1/4 cup flour

- 1/4 cup vegetable oil

- 1 cup onions diced, 1/4" cubes

- 1 cup white wine

- 1 cup chicken stock (see recipe)

- 2 Tbsp. brown sugar

- 1 tsp. black pepper, freshly ground

- 2 tsp. caraway seed

- 1 Tbsp. chicken base

- 4 cups sauerkraut

SERVES: 4

DUCK or GEESE STEW

Debone duck/goose breast and thigh meat. Remove skin, fat and silver skin. Cut into 1" cubes. In a large heavy skillet, heat oil to smoke hot. Roll duck/goose cubes in flour. Shake off excess flour. Add meat to oil and brown. Remove meat. Add onion, celery, carrots, turnips, garlic and sauté for 5 minutes. Add bay leaves, salt, pepper and remaining flour from dredging and stir gently.

Remove ingredients to a Dutch oven or large covered casserole dish. Add duck/goose cubes and remaining ingredients except for the potatoes. Combine well. Cover and bake at 350° for 1 1/2 hours. Add potatoes and stir gently from bottom. Return to oven. Bake 30 minutes or until potatoes are tender.

Serve with rice or noodles.

Chef John's Tips

- Serve with rice or noodles.
- Always check birds for shot.

Duck or Geese Stew Ingredients

- 4 cups boneless duck/goose meat, cut in 1" cubes
- 1/4 cup vegetable oil
- 1/2 cup flour
- 1 cup onions, cut in 1/2" cubes
- 1 cup celery, cut in 1/2" cubes
- 2 cups carrots, cut in 1/4" slices
- 1 cup turnips or parsnips, cut in 1/4" slices
- 2 cloves garlic, diced fine
- 2 bay leaves
- 1 tsp. salt
- 1 tsp. black pepper
- 3 cups beef stock base (see recipe)
- 3 cups diced tomatoes with juice
- 1 tsp. dried thyme
- 1/2 cup dill pickle juice
- 3 cups potatoes, peeled, cut in 1" cubes

SERVES: 4 to 6

SEARED DUCK

Ducks need to have skin on for this preparation. Remove all pin feathers and hair. Clean duck cavities well and rinse out. Pat dry inside and out with a paper towel. This step is very important to keep hot oil from boiling over when adding ducks.

In a small deep fat fryer, heat oil to 375°. Add duck, breast side down. Fry for 15 to 20 minutes. Duck is best when prepared medium rare. The last 3 minutes add chili peppers with stems, seeds removed and cut in half the long way. When duck and peppers are done, remove them to a paper-lined plate. Brush duck generously with sweet and sour sauce.

To check for doneness, make a small cut next to the breast bone. If meat is rare, return to oil a few minutes longer.

To serve, split duck in half and serve on white rice, wild rice or with a boiled potato.

Chef John's Tips

- Use any sauce you like.
- If oil is hotter than 375°, duck will burn on the outside before fully cooked on the inside. If oil is lower than 375°, duck will absorb too much oil.
- Be careful not to use peanut oil as many people are allergic to nuts.
- It is very important not to overload your deepfat fryer. If you have a small deep fat fryer, only do one duck at a time. You can hold ducks for service in a 175° oven after cooled.
- Always check birds for shot.

Seared Duck Ingredients

- *4 small ducks*
- *2 quarts vegetable oil*
- *2 to 4 medium hot chili peppers (jalapeño)*
- *1/2 cup sweet and sour sauce*

SERVES: 4

GRILLED DUCK FINGERS with CASHEW APPLESAUCE

Remove skin from duck. Cut into strips the size of your little finger.

For marinade, place all ingredients in a blender and blend for 1 minute. Place marinade in a ziplock bag with duck fingers. Refrigerate overnight.

For sauce, place all ingredients in a blender and blend smooth.

To prepare, soak skewers in water for a half hour. Stick skewers through fingers the long way. Grill on medium heat until done about 2 minutes on each side. Serve with dipping sauce.

Chef John's Tips

- You can also cook this under the broiler. Place a sheet of foil over each skewer end to keep from burning the wood.
- This recipe also works very well with red game strips. Only use the most tender cuts.
- Always check birds for shot.

Grilled Duck Fingers with Cashew Applesauce Ingredients

- 4 duck breasts (boneless and skinless)

Marinade

- 1 cup coconut flakes
- 1 Tbsp. fresh ginger, peeled and diced fine
- 2 tsp. curry powder
- 1 Tbsp. lemon juice
- 3 drops Tabasco sauce
- 1 cup orange juice

Sauce

- 1/2 cup smooth peanut butter
- 1 clove garlic
- 2 Tbsp. fresh lime juice
- 2 Tbsp. soy sauce
- 1 tsp. brown sugar
- 3 drops Tabasco sauce (or to taste)
- 1/2 cup apple sauce
- 1/2 cup cashew pieces
- 1/2 tsp. salt
- 25 - 7" bamboo skewers

SERVES: 4

GOOSE BREAST SAUTÉ

Remove skin and silver skin from goose breast. Slice into 1/4" thick slices. Flatten goose slices with a mallet. Dredge in seasoned flour. Heat clarified butter and sauté shallots until tender and clear. (Be careful not to brown.) Add goose slices and sauté 30 seconds. Simmer for 5 minutes on low heat. Add tarragon leaves and salt. Simmer for 2 minutes. Turn and sauté 30 seconds on other side. Add wine, lemon juice, brown sauce and pepper. Simmer for 5 minutes on low heat.

Serve three goose breast slices on a plate with 1/4 cup sauce. Garnish with a lemon slice, cut in half and place on side of plate with a parsley sprig.

Chef John's Tips

- This dish should be served immediately after preparation.
- You may add two cups sliced fresh mushrooms after sautéeing goose meat and before simmering for 5 minutes.
- Make sure not to flatten slices too much. There should be no holes.
- Always check birds for shot.

Goose Breast Sauté
Ingredients

- 4 goose breast slabs, cut into thin slices

- 1/2 cup seasoned flour (see recipe)

- 1 Tbsp. clarified butter (see recipe)

- 1/4 cup minced shallots

- 1/2 Tbsp. fresh tarragon

- 1 tsp. salt

- 1 cup dry white wine

- 2 tsp. fresh lemon juice

- 1/2 cup brown sauce or gravy (see recipe)

- 1/2 tsp. fresh ground black pepper

- 4 lemon slices, 1/4" thick

SERVES: 4

ROASTING WILD GEESE and DUCKS

Clean geese and ducks inside and out. Soak in cold salted water for 1 hour. Remove and drain well.

Season inside of birds with salt and pepper. Place lemon and onion pieces in the cavity. Place birds in a roasting bag. Add wine, seal bag and place in a roasting pan. Bake at 300° until birds are tender to the touch and internal temperature is 180° in the thickest part of the breast. The breast should start to separate from the breastbone.

Remove birds from the bag. Cut into desired pieces. Discard lemon, onion and juice.

Never stuff any kind of bird. The cavity is where the most bacteria are.

Chef John's Tips

- Do not cut lemon in half. The white membrane is bitter.
- For teal and small birds use smaller amounts of onion and lemon zest.
- This recipe is based on 1 large goose. For smaller geese or ducks, place additional lemon, onion, and salt in each cavity.
- Always check birds for shot

Roasting Wild Geese and Ducks Ingredients

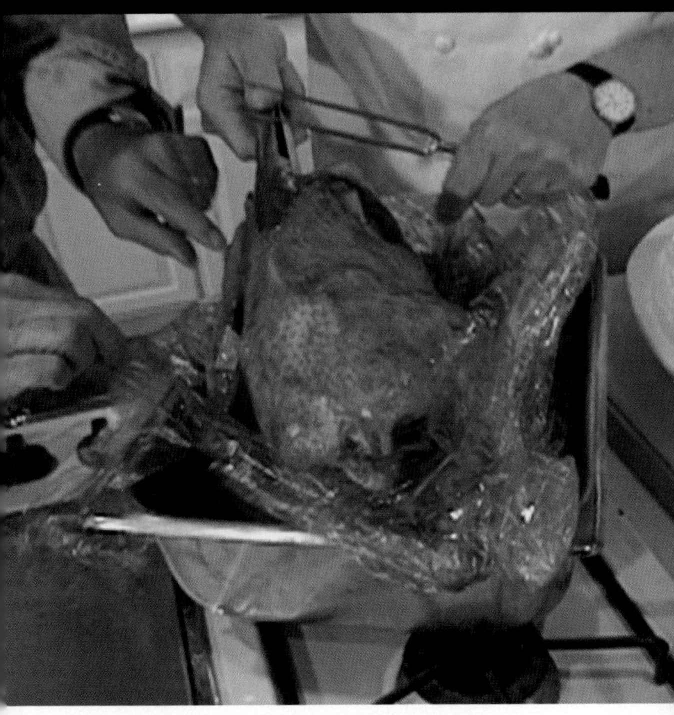

- 1 large or 2 small geese or ducks
- Salt water soak (see recipe below)
- 1 Tbsp. salt
- 1 tsp. black pepper
- 1 onion, cut into 4 pieces
- 1 lemon, whole
- 1 cup dry white wine
- 1 large roasting bag

Salt Water Soak:

- 1 gallon cold water
- 3 Tbsp. salt

SERVES: 2 hungry diners or 4 easy eaters.

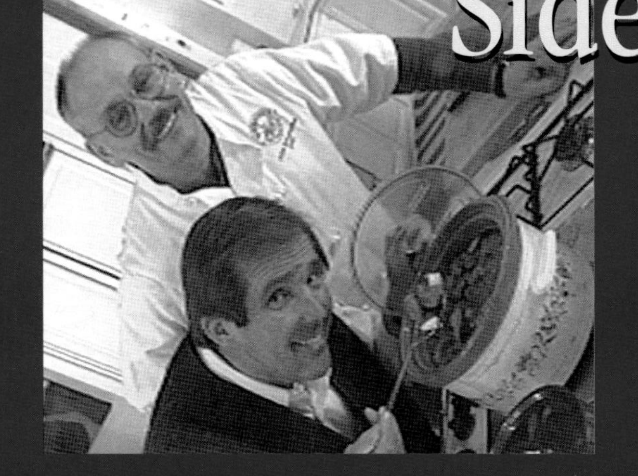

Side Dish Recipes

CHEF JOHN'S BARBECUE GAME RUB

- *1 tsp. garlic powder*
- *1 tsp. ground cumin*
- *2 Tbsp. chili powder*
- *1 tsp. freshly ground black pepper*
- *1/4 tsp. red guajillo*
- *1/4 cup Hungarian paprika*
- *2 tsp. onion powder*
- *1 tsp. dry basil*
- *1 tsp. cocoa powder*
- *1 1/2 tsp. dill seeds*
- *1 1/2 tsp. fennel seed, ground*
- *1/4 tsp. dry bay leaf*
- *1 tsp. brown mustard seeds*
- *1/2 tsp. cinnamon*
- *dry horseradish*
- *olive oil spray*

Mix all ingredients together except olive oil spray, making sure there are no lumps. Keep in tightly sealed container. For use, lightly spray meat or fowl with olive oil spray. Rub on spices. Place in a plastic bag overnight. Remove from bag and spray lightly with oil and grill. To roast, do the same as for grilling.

Chef John's Tips

- The reason to place rubbed meat in a bag overnight is to let the dry spices moisten on the outer edge of the meat.

BARBECUE COLA CHILI SAUCE

- *1 Tbsp. olive oil*
- *1 clove garlic diced fine*
- *1/2 cup onions diced fine*
- *2 tsp. red pepper flakes*
- *1 cup beef stock (see recipe)*
- *1/2 cup cola soda*
- *1/2 cup tomato chili sauce*
- *1/4 tsp. freshly ground black pepper*
- *1 tsp. Kosher salt*
- *1/3 cup tomato puree*
- *1/4 cup A-1 sauce*

In a sauce pot heat oil. Add garlic and onions and sauté until tender. Add remaining ingredients and simmer on low heat for 30 minutes uncovered.

Chef John's Tips

- This goes on all game. For some extra zip, add 1 Tbsp. fresh ginger minced fine after sauce is cooked.

BROWN MUSTARD BRANDY SAUCE

- *1/4 cup German brown mustard*
- *1/4 cup brown sugar*
- *1/2 cup Brandy*
- *1/4 cup Worcestershire sauce*
- *1/4 cup olive oil*
- *2 cloves garlic (mashed)*
- *1/2 tsp. black pepper freshly ground*

Place all ingredients in a blender and purée for 30 seconds. Place meat in a glass bowl and cover with liquid. Cover bowl tightly. I recommend marinating in meat sauce for 24 - 72 hours in the refrigerator before grilling.

Pour the leftover marinade over the meat while cooking.

CLARIFIED BUTTER

- 1 lb. butter

This is sometimes known as "drawn butter."

Place butter in a sauce pan at low heat until it is completely melted. Remove all foam which rises to the top of liquid. Take from heat, and let stand until all milk solids have fallen to the bottom of the pot. With a ladle, remove all clear oil and keep.

You may also use margarine, or one-half margarine and one-half butter. One pound of butter or margarine will yield about 12 ounces or 1 1/2 cups.

Chef John's Tips

- The best way to skim is to lightly move the ladle in a circular motion around the pot. If you use a clear glass measuring cup in the microwave, it is easy to see where the butter and milk separate.

FRESH BREAD CRUMBS

- 1 lb. loaf white bread

Remove crust from bottom of bread. Cut slices in half. Place in a food processor and make into medium to fine crumbs. A blender also works well. Add 4 half slices one at a time. Blend on medium speed to make crumbs. Remove crumbs to a bowl. Repeat until all crumbs are made.

For different flavors: use whole wheat bread, light rye bread or pumpernickel bread.

Chef John's Tips

- Making fresh bread crumbs is an important and often overlooked detail of cooking. Fresh bread crumbs are far superior to prepared crumbs which become overcooked, dry and tasteless.
- Only make as many crumbs as you need.
- Do not use leftover crumbs. You run the risk of food poisoning.
- If crumbs are refrigerated too long, they will mold.

SEASONED FLOUR

- *1 cup all-purpose flour*
- *2 tsp. salt*
- *1/2 tsp. white pepper*

Combine well.

Chef John's Tips

- The reason for using white pepper is so that the flour does not appear to have black flecks
- Never reuse excess flour

EGG WASH

- *2 eggs*
- *1/4 cup milk*

Break eggs into a bowl. Add milk. Whisk to a froth.

Chef John's Tips

- Never keep egg wash after use as it is a medium for bacteria. If you need a small amount, make half a batch.

ROOT BEER CRANBERRIES & MOUSSE

- *12 oz. Root Beer (1 can or bottle)*
- *12 oz. bag whole cranberries (fresh or frozen)*
- *1 1/2 cups sugar*
- *1 Tbsp. cornstarch*

Place root beer and cranberries in a sauce pan and bring to a boil. Mix together sugar and cornstarch and add to root beer/cranberry mixture. Simmer for 5 minutes until liquid becomes clear and shiny. Chill cranberry mixture and serve. Also can be served hot.

Chef John's Tips

- Here is a fun idea. For 4 portions of mousse, whip 2 pints heavy whipping cream (the heavier the better) until cream is stiff. Fold in 1 cup Root Beer Cranberries. In 4 tall stemmed glasses, layer the cream mixture with the Root Beer Cranberries to the desired fullness.

TOMATO SALSA

- *4 large ripe tomatoes*
- *1/4 cup olive oil*
- *1/4 cup balsamic vinegar*
- *2 cloves garlic, minced fine*
- *1 cup red onions, diced 1/4"*
- *1/2 cup green jalapeño peppers, diced 1/4"*
- *1 cup yellow or red peppers, diced 1/4"*
- *2 tsp. celery salt*
- *1 tsp. black pepper, freshly ground*
- *1 Tbsp. brown sugar*
- *1/4 tsp. hot sauce*
- *1 Tbsp. Worcestershire sauce*
- *2 tsp. fresh chopped cilantro*

Using fully ripened tomatoes, remove cores and dice into 1/2" cubes. In a small sauce pan, place olive oil, vinegar, garlic, onions, and cover tightly. Simmer on low heat for about 8 to 10 minutes. Do not boil! Remove and let cool.

Remove seeds and dice jalapeños and peppers.

In a large bowl, combine onion base with salt, pepper, sugar, hot sauce and Worcestershire sauce. Add tomatoes, peppers and cilantro and gently mix with vegetables.

Let stand for at least 2 hours and serve or refrigerate for later use.

Chef John's Tips

- There are as many ways of making salsa as stars in the sky. This is an easy way to start.
- Salsa in Spanish means "sauce."

STEAK AND CHOP RUB

- 1 Tbsp. dry basil
- 2 Tbsp. coarsely ground black pepper
- 2 Tbsp. onion powder
- 1 Tbsp. garlic powder
- 1 tsp. Hungarian paprika
- 2 tsp. dry mustard
- 2 tsp. ground ginger
- 1 tsp. ground allspice
- 1 tsp. chili powder
- olive oil

Place all ingredients, except olive oil, in a bowl and blend well. Rub on steak or chops 30 minutes before grilling. Place chops in a plastic bag with a small amount of olive oil. This softens the spices so as not to cause a burnt crust.

Chef John's Tips

- Do not put rub spices on too thick or it will burn the crust.
- There is no salt in this recipe as salt draws out moisture. Salt should only be added after cooking.

CHIPPEWA WILD RICE CASSEROLE

- *1 cup wild rice*
- *1/2 lb. sliced mushrooms*
- *3 Tbsp. shallots, minced*
- *1/2 cup sunflower seeds*
- *1 bay leaf*
- *1 tsp. Worcestershire sauce*
- *2 cups chicken stock (see recipe)*
- *1/4 cup butter*

Rinse wild rice under running water using strainer and drain. Combine rice, mushrooms, shallots, sunflower seeds, bay leaf and Worcestershire sauce in 2 quart casserole. Add broth, dot with butter, cover and bake in 350° oven until rice is tender and liquid is absorbed (about 1 1/2 hours).

Chef John's Tips

- Add two cups cooked wild rice to your favorite soup for a wild nutty flavor

HONEY SUNFLOWER CORN BREAD

- *2 large eggs, beaten*
- *1 cup Half and Half*
- *1/4 cup honey*
- *1/4 cup vegetable oil*
- *1/2 tsp. salt*
- *1/4 cup brown sugar*
- *1 cup all-purpose flour*
- *1 cup yellow cornmeal*
- *1 Tbsp. baking powder*
- *1/2 cup unsalted sunflower seeds*

SERVES: 4 to 6

In a bowl place eggs, Half and Half, honey, vegetable oil, salt and brown sugar and whisk to a froth. Combine flour, cornmeal, baking powder and sunflower seeds. Stir ingredients together just until combined well and moistened. Pour into greased 9" square baking pan. Bake at 375° for 20 to 25 minutes or until toothpick inserted comes out clean.

Eat with tons of butter and honey.

Chef John's Tips

- If you aren't a sunflower seed fan, substitute your favorite nuts or leave out the nuts altogether.

SKILLET CAMP POTATOES

- *6 cups sliced potatoes, unpeeled*
- *1 cup sliced onions*
- *1/3 cup butter, melted*
- *2 tsp. garlic salt*
- *1/4 tsp. black pepper*
- *1/2 cup shredded sharp Cheddar cheese*
- *1 cup chicken stock (see recipe)*
- *1 tsp. Worcestershire sauce*
- *1/4 cup barbecue sauce*

SERVES: 4 to 6

Wash and slice potatoes. Cut onions in half, then slice into 1/4" strips. Line a baking pan or skillet with double thickness of foil to create a foil pan. Combine potatoes, onions, butter and salt and pepper. Place in pan. Top with cheese. Add chicken stock and Worcestershire sauce. Remove foil pan from baking pan and grill over medium heat for 35 to 40 minutes, or until potatoes are tender. Sprinkle with barbecue sauce and serve.

Chef John's Tip

- If chicken stock is not available – add 1 cup water and increase barbecue sauce to 1/2 cup.

BAKING POWDER BISCUIT SQUARES

- *2 cups flour*
- *1 tsp. salt*
- *1 Tbsp. baking powder*
- *1/4 cup vegetable shortening*
- *2 Tbsp. butter*
- *2/3 cup milk*
- *1/4 tsp. pure vanilla extract*

SERVES: 4 to 6

Preheat oven to 450°. In a large mixing bowl, combine flour, salt and baking powder. Add shortening and butter. Toss mixture until it has a texture of meal. Add vanilla to milk. Sprinkle liquids evenly over base. Rub your hand with a little butter or shortening and combine mixture into a soft, puffy dough. Place dough on a lightly floured baker's cloth. Knead gently exactly 6 times. Pat dough to 1/2" thickness. Cut into 2" squares. Place on a lightly greased baking pan at 450° for 10 to 12 minutes.

Serve immediately or place in a bowl with a cotton dish towel covering the top. The cotton cloth will let the steam escape.

Chef John's Tips

- The reason I cut the biscuits into squares was to leave no dough pieces to reshape and recut.

ONE-EYED JACKS

8 slices cinnamon bread, cut 1/2" thick
1 Tbsp. butter
8 large eggs

Batter: 3 eggs
1/2 cup Half and Half
2 Tbsp. brown sugar
1 tsp. vanilla
1 tsp. cinnamon

To Make Batter: Place all ingredients in a large bowl and whisk until smooth.

Cut center from bread slices with a 3" round cutter. Heat skillet to medium hot. Add 1/2 Tbsp. butter. Dip 4 slices bread one at a time in batter shaking off excess batter. Place in pan. Break one egg in the center of each piece and fry until egg coagulates and bread is golden brown. Turn and fry to desired doneness.

Serve 2 slices per person with syrup, jam and fried apples.

Chef John's Tips

- A pop can works well as a cookie cutter.

SUBMARINE PANCAKES

- *2 cups all-purpose flour*
- *1/3 cup brown sugar*
- *1 Tbsp. baking powder*
- *1/2 tsp. salt*
- *1/2 tsp. nutmeg*
- *1/2 tsp. cinnamon*
- *1/4 cup butter*
- *1 cup Half and Half*
- *1 egg, beaten*
- *1/2 cup your favorite jam or jelly*
- *1/4 cup brown sugar*

SERVES: 4 to 6

Combine flour, sugar, baking powder, salt, nutmeg, cinnamon and sift out lumps. Let butter come to room temperature.

Place dry ingredients in a bowl except last 1/4 cup brown sugar. Add butter and mix together to the consistency of cornmeal. Add Half and Half and egg. With a large spoon stir until ingredients are just blended.

Grease a frying pan or Dutch oven and add 1 tablespoon flour. Roll flour around to coat grease and remove excess flour. Add batter. In thin lines, evenly dot top with jam.

Bake in a 400° oven for 20 to 25 minutes. To test for doneness, press the center of the cake lightly with the back of your hand. If it feels firm, it is done. If it feels mushy, return to oven for 5 minutes longer. When cake is done, immediately sprinkle last 1/4 cup sugar over the top to make glaze!

To serve, remove cake from pan. Cut into pieces and serve with butter, syrup, honey or jam.

Chef John's Tips

- For campfire baking, grease and dust a Dutch oven. Fill with batter. Cover and cook over medium heat for 15 to 20 minutes. To test for doneness, press the center of the cake lightly with the back of your hand. If it feels firm, it is done. If it feels mushy, remove from fire and let sit covered for 10 minutes. The latent heat from the pan will complete the cooking.
- If I know I am making this at camp, I combine my dry ingredients in a plastic bag. Add 1 tablespoon butter buds. When preparing at camp, I add 1/4 cup vegetable oil instead of butter.
- This is also a great snack or dessert covered with fresh fruit.

PIE CRUST

- *2 cups all-purpose flour*
- *1 tsp. salt*
- *1 1/4 cups shortening*
- *2/3 cup cold water*

Preheat oven to 350°.

In a large bowl, place flour and salt. Add shortening. Toss to make pieces the size of small marbles. Add ice cold water. Lightly toss enough to make a dough. Combine dough just enough to hold together. Use a dusted pastry cloth or board to roll out the crust.

For pie shells, dot crust with a fork. Gently shake to shrink dough. Place in pie pan and place second pie pan on top rack. Trim excess dough from edges. Place pans in oven upside down and bake at 350 ° for 15 - 18 minutes. This keeps pies from blistering and bubbling.

This will make four single-crust or two double-crust 9" pies.

Chef John's Tips

- To make double crust pies: Bottom pie crust should weigh 8 ounces. Top crust should weigh 7 ounces for a 9-inch pan. Leftover pie crust dough freezes well. Cut into proper weight and freeze in individual bags. Too much flour will make the crust tough. Always remember to shake crust after putting in a pan. This will help shrink crust before baking.

SACHET BAG

- *1 Tbsp. chopped parsley with stems*
- *1 tsp. thyme*
- *2 small bay leaves*
- *1/2 tsp. cracked black peppercorns*
- *3 crushed garlic cloves*
- *4 whole cloves*
- *cheesecloth or tea ball*

Makes one bag. The purpose of a sachet bag is to produce a balance of seasonings for stocks and soups while being able to remove all spice ingredients when desired.

Place all ingredients in a double-thick cheesecloth or tea ball. Tie cheesecloth loosely with string so the liquid can pass through and extract flavor.

ROASTED SWEET CORN

- *8 ears sweet corn*
- *2 quarts ice cold water*
- *1/4 cup vegetable oil*
- *1/2 lb. butter*
- *salt & pepper to taste*

The most important step is to find ripe ears of sweet corn with no worms. Remove corn silk and place ears in a container with cold water for at least 30 minutes.

Just before removing ears from water, add vegetable oil to water. Remove one ear at a time. This will allow the oil to coat the husk. Roast ears over medium heat (about 375°). Roast on each side for 4 minutes. Turn ear 1/3 turn and repeat until all sides are roasted. Keep a close eye on the color of the kernels. When they become an orange yellow color, the ears are ready. Do not worry if the husk becomes dark brown or black.

To eat, peel husk back. Cover corn with butter. Sprinkle kernels with salt and black pepper.

SERVES 4

Chef John's Tips

- If you have corn left over simply cut kernels from cobs with a sharp knife and keep. Reheat in butter later.
- For extra flavor, brush cooked corn with barbecue sauce, garlic butter, powdered cheddar cheese or Cajun seasoning.
- If you are taking corn on a camping trip or picnic, place corn in a plastic resealable bag with ice. This will keep the corn cold and as the ice melts the husks absorb the moisture.
- Do nut put salt in the water for soaking as salt will make the corn tough.
- After covering corn with butter, you may want to roll corn in a warm tortilla shell to keep corn warm and help in the ease of eating.

ROASTED CARROTS or PARSNIPS or NEW POTATOES

- *8 carrots or parsnips (about 6" long) or new potatoes*
- *3 cups chicken stock (see recipe)*
- *1 cup barbecue sauce*

SERVES: 4

Peel and remove end from carrots or parsnips. In a sauce pot, place chicken stock and barbecue sauce on the carrots, parsnips or potatoes. Simmer on medium heat for 15 minutes. Remove from heat and let cool in the stock.

To grill, remove vegetables from liquid. Brush or spray lightly with olive oil and grill until hot and golden brown on all sides.

Chef John's Tips

- Carrots, parsnips or potatoes should be simmered until half-cooked. They will continue to cook in the stock after removing pot from the heat.
- To take vegetables camping, after vegetables are cooked and well chilled, place vegetables in a resealable plastic bag. Add 2 oz. olive oil to keep vegetables moist and coated in oil. Keep well chilled until it is time to grill.
- For new potatoes, do not peel. Make sure to clean well with a vegetable brush before par cooking.
- The barbecue sauce in the stock adds a great flavor to the vegetables.
- Keep the liquid stock for making soup or poaching other vegetables. This stock is also excellent to precook chicken or ribs before grilling.

ROASTED SWEET PEPPERS

- *4 whole peppers of choice*
- *1 oz. olive oil*

Wash peppers well in warm water. Spray or brush a light coating of olive oil over peppers and grill on medium heat until light brown on all sides. Remove to serving platter.

ROASTED SUMMER SQUASH or ZUCCHINI

- *4 summer squash, green or yellow*
- *2 oz. olive oil*

Wash squash well in cold water and clean with a vegetable brush. Cut in half the long way. Remove stem ends. Brush or spray with olive oil. Place on medium heat on grill skin side up. Grill 3 to 4 minutes. Turn to mark. Grill 2 minutes. Turn over to cook bottom for 2 minutes. Season with salt and pepper. Remove and serve 2 slices per person.

Chef John's Tips

- Prepare acorn squash the same as summer squash only remove seeds after cutting in half.

GAME BAKING POWDER DUMPLINGS

- 1 1/2 cups all purpose flour
- 2 tsp. baking powder
- 1 tsp. salt
- 1 tsp. tarragon
- 1/4 cup butter, softened
- 3/4 cup milk

SERVES: 4 to 6

In a bowl, combine flour, baking powder, salt and tarragon. Add butter and toss to make a crumbly mixture. Add milk and stir gently to make dough. Do not over stir. Make sure there are no dry flour spots. Drop by using a teaspoon into bubbling stew. Cover and simmer for 10 minutes.

Chef John's Tips

- Before dipping the dumpling, first dip spoon in the stew. Then fill the teaspoon. Dip in hot stew and repeat.
- Do not lift the cover while cooking dumplings.

BROWN GAME STOCK OR BEEF STOCK

- 5 lbs. game or beef bones, cut into 4" pieces
- 2 1/2 cups onions, diced 1"
- 2 1/2 cups celery, diced 1"
- 1 1/2 cups carrots, diced 1"
- 1 1/2 gallons water
- 2 cups crushed tomatoes
- 1 sachet bag (see recipe)

This very important recipe will provide the base for many sauces and soups.

Wash bones and season with salt and pepper. Place in a roasting pan. Brown bones in a 375° oven for one hour, turning from time to time.

Add onions, celery and carrots and stir. Return to oven and bake until vegetables are golden brown. Remove browned bones, vegetables and drippings to a stock pot. Add water. Simmer on low heat for three hours. Remove fat and foam as they rise to the surface. Add crushed tomatoes and sachet bag. Simmer for three hours. Skim off fat and foam. Put liquid through a fine strainer. Discard bones and vegetables.

Put liquid back on stove and bring to a fast boil, reducing by one-third. Makes about 3 quarts.

Chef John's Tips

- It is best to use bones with some meat on them.
- Do not use leaves or peelings of vegetables in your soup stocks. They will give the stock a bitter taste.
- If you don't have bones, you can use 5 pounds bone-in shoulder roast.
- Beef stock can be made the same as game stock. By all means, it is alright to use premade or canned stock.

SOUPY CAMPBELL BEANS

- 1 can kidney beans (15 oz.)
- 1 can butter beans (15.5 oz.)
- 2 cans pork and beans (15 oz.)
- 1 cup brown sugar
- 1 1/4 cups onions, cut in small pieces
- 1/2 cup ketchup
- 2 tsp. yellow mustard
- 1/3 cup dill pickle juice
- 1/4 cup maple syrup

Drain kidney beans and butter beans. Place all ingredients into a heavy pot. Simmer uncovered on low heat for 45 minutes or until onions are tender, stirring gently to keep from sticking.

Chef John's Tips

- I got this recipe in the submarine service from my leading cook, Soupy Campbell. These are great beans-hot or cold!
- You can also add ground game. For my kids, I brown 2 pounds ground venison, drain the fat and add to beans. My family calls this "Slumgovia."

GRANDMA SCHUMACHER'S HASH BROWNS

- *6 cups grated raw potatoes*
- *2 tsp. fresh lemon juice*
- *1/2 cup onions, diced 1/4"*
- *1/2 cup heavy cream*
- *1 tsp. salt*
- *1/2 tsp. white pepper*
- *1/4 cup butter*

SERVES: 4

Grate or shred potatoes. Put potatoes and lemon juice in a bowl, and let sit for 10 minutes. Drain off excess liquids. Add onions, cream, salt and pepper and mix.

In a medium, non-stick frying pan, bring butter to a fast bubble. Add potato batter and cover. Cook on medium heat until potatoes are brown. Turn potatoes, cover, and steam through. Potatoes should be light brown on both sides. Remove from pan and cut into squares.

Chef John's Tips

- Be careful not to use too large a frying pan. Potato squares should be about two inches thick. If using an electric frying pan, cut potato cake in quarters before turning.

CHEF JOHN'S HORSERADISH

- *5 cups shredded horseradish*
- *1/2 cup cold water*
- *1 1/2 cups white wine vinegar*
- *1/2 tsp. white pepper*
- *1/2 cup sugar*
- *1 jalapeño pepper, sliced 1/4"*

Wash and peel horseradish roots with a potato peeler. Shred in a bowl. Add water, vinegar, white pepper and sugar and combine well. Remove seeds and stem from pepper. Slice into pieces and add to base. Place in a covered container. Let stand for 3 days and stir. Use and enjoy.

Chef John's Tips

- I like the texture of shredding. You can chop in a Cusinart or grind horseradish if you wish. To make horseradish hotter, add more white pepper and another jalapeño pepper.
- Make sure to keep this covered in the refrigerator!
- This is my secret recipe. Do not share this with anyone.

HORSERADISH SAUCE

- *1/2 cup John's horseradish (see recipe)*
- *1 tsp. Worcestershire sauce*
- *1 1/2 cups mayonnaise*
- *3 Tbsp. sugar*
- *3 drops Tabasco Sauce*

Chop John's horseradish fine and strain off excess liquid. Place all ingredients in a bowl and combine very well. Keep in a glass container and refrigerate.

YIELDS: 2 cups

CHEF JOHN'S "Good Eatin" COBBLER

1 1/2 cups brown sugar
1 1/2 Tbsp. cornstarch
1 Tbsp. non-dairy creamer
1 Tbsp. non-fat dry milk
1/2 tsp. nutmeg
1/2 tsp cinnamon
2/3 cup raisins
1 - 12 oz. can soda (any flavor)
4 cups fresh fruit + liquid from fruit
Biscuits (see recipe)

FRUIT BASE:
Combine all dry ingredients and sift. Place in a resealable plastic bag. Add raisins and close tight.

TO MAKE FRUIT FILLING:
In a Dutch oven, pour a 12-oz. can of soda. Bring to a brisk boil. Add fresh fruit and return to a boil. Add dry base and with a wooden spoon stir well to combine. Spoon biscuits over the top. Cover and bake in a 375° oven or over campfire coals for 30 minutes.

FOR DUTCH OVEN COOKING OVER A CAMPFIRE:
Place Dutch oven over white hot coals (about 3" to 4" above coals). If lid is concave, place 5 to 7 hot coals on the lid. Let bake for 30 minutes. Check for doneness.

Cobbler is done when biscuits are baked through. To test for doneness, when a little piece is broken off, the inside should be white and look like a sponge.

There are so many variables when checking for doneness. Start after about 20 minutes with variables. It could take less or more time depending on the altitude, outside temperature, thickness of Dutch oven and heat source of fire.

CORN BREAD STUFFING

- *1/2 cup salted butter*
- *1 1/2 cups red onions, cut 1/4"*
- *2 cloves garlic, minced fine*
- *1 cup celery, cut in 1/4" slices*
- *1 cup yellow or red pepper, cut in 1/4" cubes*
- *1/2 cup sweet gherkin pickles, cut in 1/4" cubes*
- *1/4 cup sunflower seeds*
- *6 cups cubed corn bread, pieces cut in 1/2" cubes*
- *3 eggs beaten*
- *1 cup game or beef stock (see recipe)*
- *2 tsp. thyme*
- *1 tsp. tarragon*
- *1 tsp. dry poultry seasoning*
- *2 tsp. Worcestershire sauce*
- *1/2 tsp. salt*
- *1/2 tsp. freshly ground black pepper*
- *1 cup fresh pears, peeled, cut in 1/2" cubes*

SERVES: 1 1/2 quarts

Preheat oven to 350°. In a large skillet, heat butter to a fast bubble. Add onions, garlic, celery, peppers and sauté until onions are tender. Add pickles and sunflower seeds. Turn heat to low and simmer 10 minutes. Place in a large mixing bowl. Add corn bread and toss to combine. Do not over mix.

(Recipe continued on next page.)

CORN BREAD STUFFING (cont.)

In a large bowl, place eggs, game stock, spices, Worcestershire sauce, salt and pepper. Whisk to combine well. Add pears and corn bread mixture. Combine well. Place in a Dutch oven or covered baking dish. Bake stuffing in a 350° oven for about 1 hour.

VARIATIONS:

MARYLAND STYLE: Add 2 cups raw oysters and liquid as a last step. Very gently fold in the stuffing.

SOUTHWESTERN STYLE: Add deseeded hot chili peppers cut in 1/4" cubes.

HEARTLAND STYLE: Add 1 cup pork sausage with vegetables in first step.

CANADIAN STYLE: Add 1 1/2 cups smoked salmon pieces as the last step.

Chef John's Tips

- Excess stuffing can be frozen in double thick resealable plastic bags.
- If you are not a fan of sunflower seeds, substitute walnut pieces.

BISCUITS

- 2 1/2 cups biscuit mix
- 1/2 cup dry potato flakes or pearls
- 2 Tbsp. non-fat dry milk
- 2 Tbsp. non-dairy creamer
- 1/2 tsp. nutmeg
- 1 tsp. baking powder
- 1 cup very cold water

In a one-gallon size plastic resealable bag, place all dry ingredients and seal tightly.

TO MAKE BISCUITS FOR COBBLER:
Add 1 cup cold water to bag and knead mixture in the bag 30 times. Open bag. With a tablespoon, scoop out heaping spoons of dough. Place on top of cobbler filling. Make sure to leave room for biscuits to rise so they do not stick together. Cover pot and bake at 400° for 30 minutes.

Chef John's Tips

- It is a must to have a heavy cast iron Dutch oven or a pot the same thickness and weight as a Dutch oven.
- When baking over a campfire, do not put Dutch oven over open flames as that will burn the fruit base.
- If you wish, water works just as well as soda.
- Do not use diet soda as it has no sugar.
- I like to add 1 teaspoon ground vanilla beans to biscuit mix as they will keep well with the dry mix.
- Canned fruit works well. Substitute liquid from fruit and use it instead of water. You can add water to be sure you have 1 cup of liquid.
- The biscuit dough is the same as for making biscuits alone. To make biscuits, simply brush Dutch oven with oil or butter. Form biscuits and bake at 400° for 20 minutes covered.

(Tips continued on next page.)

Biscuit Tips continued

- Kinds of fruit - all kinds of melons (with no seeds), apples, pears, peaches, strawberries, blueberries, raspberries, plums, pineapple, cherries. If you use rhubarb, add 3/4 cup extra sugar. This recipe can be made with peeled, seeded and diced winter squash or pumpkins. For this variation, add 1/2 teaspoon ground cloves.

ROUX

Sauces and gravies are two of the most important components of great cooking. Roux thickens sauces and gravies. Although roux is only one of many cooking thickeners, I have concluded it is the best after 20 years of professional cooking.

- 1 lb. butter or margarine

- 1 lb. flour

In a heavy two-quart sauce pot or baking dish, melt butter, stir in flour, and bake for one hour at 375°. Stir the mixture every 15 minutes. When cooked, the roux should be golden brown and the consistency of sand.

It is always better to use roux at room temperature. The roux keeps well in the refrigerator or freezer.

Chef John's Tips

- You should weigh the flour for this recipe and not measure it.

BARBECUE-STUFFED CAMP POTATOES

4 large Idaho baking potatoes
1 cup shredded farmer cheese
1/2 cup barbecue sauce
1 tsp. onion salt
1/2 tsp. black pepper

SERVES 4

Wash potatoes and scrub well with a vegetable brush to remove all soil. With an apple corer, remove a plug lengthwise from the center of potatoes. In a bowl, combine shredded cheese, barbecue sauce, onion salt and black pepper. Evenly stuff center of potatoes.

Wrap potatoes tightly in a double thickness of aluminum foil. Bake on campfire or grill until potatoes are tender when pressed. You can bake the potato in a 375° oven for 1 hour. Remove from foil and serve with sour cream.

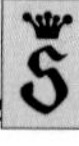

Chef John's Tips

- It is very important to scrub potatoes well as soil contains bacteria.
- Replace a small piece of potato plug on each end to seal potatoes.
- If you wish, you can add additional barbecue sauce to the outside of the potato before closing foil.

ROASTED GARLIC

- 4 bulbs garlic
- 1/3 cup olive oil
- 1 tsp. rosemary
- 1 tsp. thyme
- 1/4 tsp. salt
- 1/4 tsp. fresh ground pepper
- foil

TO PREPARE:
Slice 1/8" off the top end of head of garlic. Place a double thick sheet of foil flat on the counter. Place garlic head cut end up in the center of the foil. Turn edges of foil up to start making a bundle. Top garlic with oil, spices, salt and pepper. Close up bundle and bake at 325° for 3 hours.

Serve with fresh bread and all kinds of game.

Chef John's Tips

- This is the best way to use garlic. Once you try this recipe, you will be spoiled for life.

BROWN SAUCE

- *3 oz. butter or margarine*
- *1 cup onions, diced 1/4"*
- *1/2 cup celery, diced 1/4"*
- *1/2 cup carrots, diced 1/4"*
- *2/3 cup flour*
- *6 cups beef stock or game stock double strength (see recipe)*
- *1/4 cup tomato purée*
- *1 bay leaf*
- *1 tsp. salt*
- *1/2 tsp. black pepper*

TO PREPARE:
In a heavy sauce pot, heat butter to fast bubble, and sauté vegetables until onions are clear. Add flour and cook two minutes on low heat, stirring often with a wooden spoon or rubber spatula.

Heat stock and add to base, stirring slowly and constantly.

Add tomato purée, bay leaf, salt and pepper, and cook 30 minutes. Adjust flavor and consistency to taste. Strain through a fine strainer and serve.

Chef John's Tips

- To make double strength stock, reduce 12 cups to six cups by rapidly boiling in a large sauce pan. If you don't have homemade stock, you can use canned broth.
- This is the best base for brown gravy. If you have any left over, freeze it in one-cup amounts in freezer bags. As you need more gravy, let bags unthaw in refrigerator, heat and serve.

SCHUMACHER HOTEL SWEET ROLL STUFFING

- 12 cups dry sweet rolls, doughnuts, pastries or breads, cut in 1" cubes
- poultry parts
- 2 cups onion, diced 1/2"
- 2 cups celery, diced 1/2"
- 2 bay leaves
- 2 quarts water
- 1/2 cup butter
- 2 cloves garlic, minced fine
- 12 oz. sausage meat
- 1 tsp. thyme
- 2 tsp. poultry seasoning
- 1 tsp. sage
- 1 tsp. black pepper
- 1 cup eggs
- 1/2 cup milk
- 1 1/2 tsp. chicken base
- 2 cups chicken stock (see recipe)

TO PREPARE:
Cube sweet rolls, doughnuts, pastries or breads (dark or white) of any kind.

Boil poultry parts including neck, heart, gizzard and wings with one cup chopped onion, one cup chopped celery, two bay leaves and two quarts of water. Boil until meat is tender and is ready to fall off the bone. Strain, and remove poultry parts and pick meat from wings and neck. Combine with heart and gizzard. Cool and grind. Save stock (Do not use poultry livers. Save these for pâté).

(Recipe continued on next page.)

SCHUMACHER HOTEL SWEET ROLL STUFFING (continued)

Melt butter to a fast bubble in a frying pan. Add remaining onions and celery. And garlic and sauté until transparent. Add sausage. Cover and cook until sausage is done. Set aside to cool.

Blend spices, eggs, milk, chicken base and 2 cups chicken stock together with a wire whip. Place all ingredients in a large bowl and let sit for 20 minutes. Mix gently to combine. Be careful not to over mix and lose the identity of the various cubes.

Bake separately (fowl can carry bacteria in their cavities) in a covered, buttered baking dish for 2 1/2 hours at 350°

Chef John's Tips

- To accumulate enough cubes for this recipe, you may cube and freeze leftover pastries. When using frozen cubes, be sure to thaw completely.
- For a Central European fruit stuffing, add 1/2 cup apples, 1/2 cup pears, 1/2 cup prunes, all diced large, and 1/4 cup raisins to the recipe. Bake and serve.

CHICKEN STOCK

- *3 1/2 lb. chicken wings or 1 small stewing hen*
- *2 cups diced onions*
- *1 1/2 cups diced celery*
- *1 1/2 cups diced carrots*
- *4 quarts water*
- *1 sachet bag (see recipe)*

MAKES 4 quarts

TO PREPARE:
Wash chicken. Place all ingredients in a large soup pot and simmer on low heat for 3 1/2 hours, skimming off fat and foam from time to time. Remove from heat and strain.

Put only the liquid back in the pot and return to a fast boil until liquid has been reduced by one-half. Skim off fat, strain, cool and store.

Chef John's Tips

- Remove meat from bones and use for sandwiches and salads.

CURRY POWDER

- *1/4 cup coriander seeds*
- *2 Tbsp. cumin seeds*
- *1 Tbsp. 3 pepper blend peppercorns*
- *2 cinnamon sticks, crushed*
- *1 Tbsp. turmeric*
- *2 tsp. whole cardamom seeds*
- *1 tsp. whole cloves*
- *1 tsp. whole allspice seeds*
- *2 tsp. fennel seeds*
- *1 tsp. brown mustard seeds*
- *1 tsp. dried chili pepper, stemmed and seeded*
- *1 tsp. ground ginger*

TO PREPARE:
Place all ingredients except ground ginger in a metal baking pan. Roast at 300° for 7 minutes (not one minute longer or it will make spices bitter). Transfer to a plate. Let spices cool. When spices have cooled, grind spices to a fine powder in a spice or coffee grinder. Combine with ground ginger. Store in a sealed glass jar away from heat and light.

Chef John's Tips

- Dried chili peppers hotness scale of 1 (mild) to 10 (very hot)
  1. guajillo 2-4
  2. ancho 3-5
  3. habanero 10
- If you want mild curry powder, leave out chili peppers

POPPYSEED DRESSING

- 1 cup sugar
- 1 tsp. salt
- 1/2 tsp. white pepper
- 2 tsp. dry mustard
- 1/2 cup white vinegar
- 2 cups vegetable salad oil
- 1/4 cup onions
- 2 Tbsp. fresh lemon juice
- 3 Tbsp. poppy seeds

TO PREPARE:
Place all ingredients, except poppy seeds, in a blender container. Blend one minute. Remove from blender, add poppy seeds and mix well.

This dressing keeps refrigerated up to two weeks. Always shake well before using. My poppy seed dressing goes especially well with spinach, Boston, or Bibb lettuces.

VIDEOS

Fish and Game Cooking Made Easy
Watch and learn as Chef John & TV host Ron Schara lead you step by step through great ways of preparing wild game and fish.
Video; includes printed recipes. Price: **$12.95**

Fish Cooking Made Easy
Learn to create interesting and exceptionally tasty dishes with this amazingly versatile and often underestimated food.
Video. Price: **$12.95**

Delicious Morning Meals
In this video, Chef John shows you quick, simple and tasty ways to prepare fish for breakfast.
Video. Price: **$12.95**

A Taste of Wild Game: Camp Cooking
Join Chef John as he demonstrates his techniques of Camp cooking in a friendly, engaging and easy to follow manner.
Video. Price: **$12.95**

A Taste of Wild Game: Grilling
This video is the perfect companion for the outdoor chef. Learn the techniques of the Game Gourmet, Chef John Schumacher, as he teaches you the simple secrets to successful grilling.
Video. Price: **$12.95**

A Taste of Wild Game: Venison
The joy of the hunt can be significantly enhanced when you learn the secrets to preparing and cooking venison the Game Gourmet way!
Video. Price: **$12.95**

A Taste of Wild Game: Game Feast
On this video Chef John prepares three complete game feasts, including breakfast, lunch and dinner. Create your own "game feast" with the knowledge you gain from this video.
Video. Price: **$12.95**

A Taste of Wild Game: Jerky, Sausage and Slow Cooked Venison
Join Chef John in this informative video and learn how to make your own jerky and sausage.
Video. Price: **$12.95**

Big Game Field Care and Butchering
This twin pack of videos shows you how to field dress your animal and butcher your game at home. It also includes cutting roasts, steaks and proper grinding.
Price: **$14.95**

Items in stock are usually shipped within 5 business days. If paying by check or money order, please allow extra delivery time for them to clear. Sorry we cannot ship to P.O. Boxes, nor deliver C.O.D.

ALL ITEMS SHIPPED 4th CLASS.
Shipping + handling costs additional.
Minnesota residents add 6 1/2% sales tax.